Sufani Weisman-Gar.

The Great Gathering
of Gods Soul

Sufani Weisman-Garza

The Great Gathering of Gods Soul

About This Book

This book was written in 2003. In 2007 it was picked up by an agent and held for two years, trying to get it sold to a publisher. Although there were a few very interested publishers, it was never sold due to the dilemma on how to market it. This book touches on the global and universal needs of human beings, the questions we have about God, love, and the world we live in. In today's climate, this message is said to be even more relevant, with a more willing and open audience to discuss the problems of the world and how to fix them. You will laugh, cry and feel spiritually out of body in this devastatingly honest book about people, love and God. It has now been twenty years since I wrote this, and it has found its way into your hands, finally. It was waiting for the right time. And the time is now! Thank you!

The Great Gathering of Gods Soul

Sufani has written over a dozen books throughout her life, has been published in many print and digital magazines for health, wellness, and spirituality. She writes fiction, non-fiction and is a prolific writer. She is certified in Health Education, Cognitive Behavioral Therapy, Eastern & Western Medicine, Massage Therapy, Reiki, Shamanism, and is a Spiritual Counselor and Soul Care Provider. She has owned her own Healing Academy for over twenty years and continues as Place of Bliss Academy's Owner and Director, teaching online classes (www.placeofblissacademy.com), with over twenty-Thousand Students and over thirty-thousand enrollments. She is a Mother to three grown children and a Soul Mate to her husband of over eighteen years. She rescues animals and has a deep love for senior animals especially. She is happy!

Sufani Weisman-Garza

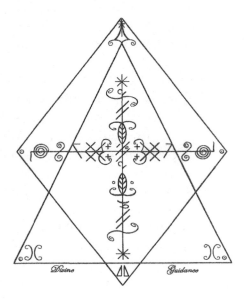

The Great Gathering of Gods Soul

The Great Gathering of Gods Soul

Table of Contents

Chapter One

Life Is But A Dream

Life could be such a dream--and in his dreams he was someone special. He was alone in a land so beautiful and there existed no such thing as loneliness. He was surrounded by pink weeping willows and the grounds were brilliant shades of green on a hilly grass top. The grass ran for as far as the eye could see. The sky was a magnificent orange glow with the yellow sun cascading its light against it. He walked slowly and with no determination but was infinitely lost in the intoxicating beauty and the sweet smell of honeysuckle flowers.

In the distance there was a white country house that rested atop the highest part of the hill that led to a lake. The generous lake shared its grace with swans and mother ducks nursing their young, near the crest of the water. It was perfection at its best and he felt complete peace while immersed in nature. As he looked over toward the house on the hill there was someone there on the big open porch sitting on a rocking chair. He wondered who it could be. He could see that it was a tall man, with brown shoulder length hair, dressed in white linen, who was waving happily to him. At that moment he knew there was no better place to be than in that moment. He felt nature's connection to him and how it must feel to be loved by someone of the world. There would be no greater gift than to give love and to be loved in return.

Slowly, he woke from his deep trance-like sleep to find yet another typical chilly winter morning in Manzanillo, Mexico, a place not of his original descent. Quickly, he got up and started to dress himself and began to long for something to look forward to. He was just a young boy with little to contribute to the world but surely he too deserved to feel the joys of a child. He brushed his teeth and tried to remember to do all the things he was supposed to do in the morning. He would do anything to keep *her*, his mother, from yelling at him.

If I just remember to be quiet and do everything right then maybe today she will love me and show me some kindness. I have been especially good this week, he thought to himself. Then a hard knock came on the door.

"Get up," she said loudly.

He opened the door as she rushed past in a hurry. He had to eat breakfast before school, and so he went into the kitchen, got a bowl of cereal, and poured the milk into the bowl. Other children at school had the *Breakalator* in their house, which came equipped with assorted cereals, milk and materialized the bowl, all in one. But he and his mother didn't have much money, so they were still doing things manually.

As he lifted the heavy gallon of milk, it came out with quickness and overflowed onto the table and all over his mother's favorite tablecloth. As he looked up at her he knew what was to come. He put the milk down and lowered his head as he threw a dishrag over the mess hoping to soften the blow that was coming.

"Look what you've done, you stupid, stupid boy," she screamed in Spanish. "Get out of here and go to school. You're nothing but trouble to me."

As he rushed out of the kitchen and into his room to collect his things for school, his eyes welled up with tears and the water expelled from his eyes and rolled down his cheek. He was filled with panic and his heart was aching in pain for the love he wished his mother felt for him but didn't.

"I hate you," she shouted at her eleven-year-old son. He had experienced her rage for years and still had not gotten used to it. He ran towards his room to gather his things and she added, "I wish you had never been born."

She was a spiritually void woman with the appearance of withered skin and her features were sharp and hard looking. She looked brazen and joyless. Her personality was sour and her spirit unkind. She had hair like wire that hung down wildly around her face as she screamed at him in anger. She had the look of cold coal in her eyes when she spoke to him as though she were the anti-love.

The Great Gathering of Gods Soul

With total despair he grabbed his coat from his room and rushed to leave before she could hurl more harsh verbal blows. But before he left his room he stopped at his window and was drawn to gaze out at the silver sky, as he always was. The window dripped with the moisture from the heat of the house and the cold of the outside world. But to him it was far colder inside his home than any outside weather could ever be. The streets were softer than the harshness of his mother. Not even the beauty of the aquamarine lagoons, wild life, or the golden sands that ran along the Pacific coast of his home could erase the hell that he lived in. All he could see was the narrowness of the life he lived.

As he walked to school, thoughts filled his head, wondering why his mother was so cold and why she treated him the way she did. He noticed how all the other children made similar mistakes without such harsh reprimands and reproaches from their parents.

He wondered why she hated him so much when he tried so hard to be good. When he was a baby she had given him love, so why did that change? But there was never an answer for him.

Lonely, sad thoughts filled his mind through his journey to school, but his friends always had a way of changing his reality back to playfulness again. He walked through the blue awnings of the markets, which ran up the hill along the broken, yet paved streets of their lower, middle-class town. Although modern civilization had created many conveniences, many of the residents that lived in Manzanillo refused to change. And they were not alone, many other proud cultures around the world were also holding on to their traditions. The Markets were a place where women could socialize with the other traditional women, and could share recipes and pride, for house and home. Perhaps that was why his mother had avoided the market and made him do most of the shopping. While the rest of the world enjoyed the benefits of self-serve shopping and robotic police who would catch the shoplifters, the little town in which he lived was stuck in the past.

14

The Great Gathering of Gods Soul

On the way to school, he was stopped by a loud melodic sound of the winged messengers of God. He looked up at the tall, immense tree to see it was not the sound of only one quetzal bird singing, but the sound of more than he could number, in an old dead avocado tree. So many had gathered in one tree as if it were a celebration. He became absorbed with their energy, their joy and their sense of community and closeness. Their feelings of joy transferred to him, and he knew there was goodness in the world. There had to be. He watched how the birds would all quiet their singing at the same time and then fly off the tree in a half circle, return quickly back to the tree and begin singing again. He wondered to himself why they did that and then was reminded by one of the children passing by that he'd better hurry up before he was late for school.

"The school bell is going to ring in a minute, Satya, you better run," the boy said as he ran past him.

Satya smiled at the boy and looked up again at the tree and began walking. He had learned to deprogram his barcode I.D long ago, when they let go of all the human teachers and installed the A.H.E., Automated-Holographic-Educators. He thought about his life before, in Venezuela, and remembered happier times when his father was still alive. While walking he kept looking back at the birds and the tree trying to keep that feeling the birds gave him of complete happiness. He felt like he had been given a gift that the birds shared with him. No one else had seen the beauty in what he had just witnessed. The short walk through the streets made him feel free and he caught his breath on the walk to school and tried to forget the cruelty he had just received at home.

On the streets, he could act like a child and the streets would not call him horrible names. He thought about being old enough to be free of his wicked mother and how he would surely run for his life and never look back. He prayed daily to God to take him far away from his life of not being wanted and give him a purpose. He needed to make a difference in his world of forgotten joy and ample soberness. He wanted to recreate a world that returned to natural affection and laughter.

He wondered if being an adult meant that he must lose the beam of light from his face the way his mother's face had lost its light. He prayed that he might find happiness and the love that others had. His life was not yet his own and he struggled to hold on to the idea that his world could change. He struggled, trying not to succumb to the harshness of life. He begged God to be with him and not let his inner light burn out under the pressure of his tumultuous life. He was fearful most of the woman who was supposed to protect him but instead lashed him with vile words and drew blood in his heart, seen only by the angels because he hid his pain. The blows were so deep to his soul that it could not be repaired, even with modern medicine. Only God could heal such wounds of a young man's soul.

He remembered the silver sky that he saw from his bedroom window and how the sun broke through the clouds. How he was filled with the shadow of hope despite his misery. It was as though he had no mother at all because a mother was there to love a child, and she gave him none. Then, just as he entered the campus he heard the terrifying squawk of a Harpy Eagle, the revered eagle of resurrection that he had learned about in school, and he knew it was a sign of something to come. Some kind of change in his life perhaps.

Later, when the school day was done, he walked back into the reality of his life. Evenings were not as bad as long as he could pray and bring his mind to a state of dream and leave his body to another world. He would go to Heaven or what he imagined it to be, and in his mind, it was far better than how the Catholic religion, the most prevalent religion in Manzanillo, expressed it. So, every day he would do his homework, rush to do his chores and clean up the house to bring some level of comfort to his mother in the hopes that she would leave him alone. He would go out into the back yard and climb into the tree house that he had worked on with his father before he died. He would reminisce how happy he was when his father was there to protect him. His mother was afraid of heights, and it was the one place he knew that she would not go to disturb him.

16

One day after school he climbed the ladder up the tree and went into his secret shelter. He decorated the walls of his little tree house when his father was alive with torn out pages from magazines that he and his father had collected of beautiful landscapes, worldly places and other things that to him could only be real in a dream world. There were pictures of exciting statues that seemed to give off wisdom and strength, although he did not totally understand the origin of their spirit world. He read books in his tree house on everything he could get his hands on to learn more. He read of famous people throughout history, good and bad. He read of fabulous places and cultures that believed in Buddha, Krishna and Jesus' goodness, generosity, love and compassion, which he found to be very powerful. He learned about Solomon's wisdom and his journey through insanity and back. Satya took deep breaths of relaxation and felt the fresh air that blew through his private house in the sky.

Slowly his body became light and weightless, and he felt his spirit separate from his body and he became free in the world he created. He opened his eyes and the sky looked bluer than before and the clouds had dispersed. The bronze sun burst into the little tree house room, and he heard a voice from below yell out,

"Son, come out here. Come down, I want to show you something."

Satya looked out of the window of the tree house and saw his father. With joy to see him he rushed to the ladder and plummeted down it.

"Look what I made," his father said smiling at him and pointing out his creation.

"Wow," Satya yelled out. "That's cool, Dad." It was a life size statue of an Indian man carved out of a dead tree in the back yard. They looked at each other and laughed.

"She's going to be mad, Dad," Satya said, speaking of his mother and looking at his dad.

"Yeah," his father said as if the thought brought him joy, and they laughed together. Then his father said, "Look what it can do. Go on, walk past it and tell me what you notice."

Satya walked in front of it, then past it, staring directly at its eyes. To his surprise, as he walked, the Indian's eyes followed him.

"How did you do that, Dad?" Satya said with excitement and joy.

"I carved the eye sockets in, instead of out. That way they follow you wherever you walk. Pretty neat, huh?"

Satya just smiled at his father, and they stood there for a moment, silently gazing at the statue. When the moment had passed Satya looked up at his father and the expression on his face turned serious. With solemn eyes he looked at his father and asked, "Father, why doesn't she love me?" As the words came out of his mouth the tears flowed from his eyes because he knew he was safe with his father. He did not sob the way other children did, with loud expression, because there was never any softness to meet with his tears from his mother. Only more harshness, so he cried, silently. He felt a pain that a child should never know. His father grabbed him and hugged him tightly as if he wished to shield him from the wickedness of his mother.

"I tried desperately to soften the woman before I crossed over son, but she had become so vile all the time. It was as if someone had stolen her soul and poured poison in her." After his father hugged him to calm his tears, he knelt down to Satya's level and talked to him with deep consolation.

"My son," he said gently holding Satya's chin in his hand. "Anger lodges in the bosom of fools. Keep forgiving her because she is sick in her soul. It isn't that she doesn't love you. She does not love even herself and therefore cannot love another being. She must first looks within to fix what has gone wrong in her own life. I know that forgiving her is hard to do," he said while taking a deep breath, "but keep forgiving her, son, for she does not know what she is doing. If she were not sick in her soul she would not act the way she does towards you. She would not hurt you the way she does."

"Have I done anything wrong, Father?"

"Not a thing, Son. She cannot accept anyone because she does not accept herself. She hates all because she hates her own skin. And neither you, nor I, were responsible then, nor are we responsible now, for her actions. You cannot save her, she must save herself," he said. "But set the example by showing her compassion," he continued as he smiled into Satya's eyes. "For, the wicked will lie of your goodness, but you will know in your heart that no wrong deed was done on your part. You will have loved in the face of hatred and your conscience will be clean. Pray for her tormented soul son," he said lovingly.

His father's eyes were like an ocean of hope for him, blue and mesmerizing. His father was a balance between two worlds that he struggled to live between. The physical world and the one of his dreams, which was his saving grace.

"You are special, Satya. Do you know why I chose your name?" his father asked.

"Why?" Satya asked.

"Because Satya means, *One who sees the true reality of things as they are, not as we would have them be.* You see truth even when it is painful and many cannot do that, Son, others cannot achieve that level of honesty, in their whole lives You see pain and do not look away. You learn from it and that is exactly as it is written for you to do. You will use your pain to help others some day. Remember that life is bittersweet, and you would not learn, grow or even know what good is if you had no contrast of its opposite. Do you understand?" his father asked.

"Yes," Satya said as he struggled to comprehend.

"You have a special gift that you can use to help others. Learn from your pain and find the hidden meaning. Never waste your pain. It is an opportunity to go deep within your soul and find your power."

Satya had never thought of his pain in that way before but quickly realized that it was true. He had always found his determination and strength in the pain of his spirit, and as a young man, he knew himself more than his mother ever would. His father's words were profound and hard for a young boy to decipher but he understood more than most, three times his age. He remembered everything that was said to him and for the parts he could not fathom, he had faith in, knowing that in the future it would be revealed to him.

"Thank you, Father," Satya said. "You know, Mother said that I would grow up to see how horrible the world is and then I would be just like her. She said that I would realize how the world maneuvers, and I'd have to remove knives from my back for the rest of my life. She said that I would never stop pulling knives out of my back. Why does she say that Father? I don't understand and I fear asking her the meaning."

"This is a metaphor, Son. It is a phrase that your mother has used to describe betrayal; People betraying her trust and hurting her."

"Oh," Satya said looking down trying to understand. "Why would people betray me? Is this what adults do to each other?" he asked.

"Not all adults, Son. People make mistakes. The world is a scary place, I will not deny that, but the world is also full of wonder, and your perception of the world is how your world will be. You can choose to focus on the bad or choose to see the good that is still prevalent. Only you determine your focus. The world is in a decadent state it is true," he said and looked deeply into Satya's eyes. "But *you* can make a difference," he said and smiled. His father knelt down before him and reached out for his hands. He held them in his hand and said gravely, "I know what you fear, Satya."

Satya returned the look to him.

"You feel as if you are the only one on the earth like you and that you will walk your entire journey through life alone. Am I right?" he asked.

Satya looked at him and the pit in his stomach became alive with distress. His father was right. His father knew the very private feelings and thoughts that had lived only in his mind and had never reached his lips to say the words. He had no one to say them to and had never heard them out loud but now that it was said, it was truer than ever.

20

His father continued,   "You feel you don't fit in anywhere and Satya, my son, I will not lie to you to spare your feelings," his father said. "You are an original, the only one of your kind. You are a precious gem, my son, because you are the truth and you face what is, whatever that may be. You are what we call on this side, an absolute. You cannot be conditioned to this world because you are not of the world." Then his father's voice became sensitive and soft. "When you accept your place in this universe the longing to be part of the masses will cease and you will know a greater peace than I can ever describe to you. Perhaps some day when your work is through, you can explain it to me," he said and then began to fade from Satya's sight.

The meditation came to an end and his father vanished. Teary-eyed, he returned to his physical reality in the tree house. He felt alone in the world and vulnerable to its badness, as his father had said. The person who was to protect him hated him the most. He felt the joy of playing with his peers at school who adored him, but all the while he still felt isolated from them. He felt like a third wheel and longed to be like everyone else. But this time his father had acknowledged a truth within him, one he had known all along, and he could no longer ignore it. He was afraid at the uncertainty of his life.

He felt changed by his father's words and felt a sort of calm he had not felt before. As though his father had shared a secret of self-preservation with him, which was needed desperately to help shape his young mind into believing there was more to life than his misery. He felt strong now, as though his mother could not destroy him, and he felt understood and accepted by his father. He understood that to survive his mother's betrayal of love, he must love her in return and show her compassion even when she was wicked. It was the only way to secure his survival. If he did not do this, she would surely win and smother his spirit, and he refused to let anyone do that.

Later that night something unusual happened-- something he would never forget. He went to bed and fell asleep thinking about the words of his father. Exhausted, he fell into a deep slumber. A dream occurred as it had so many times before.

He was in a white room and there was an immense square in the middle of the room on the floor. As he began to float upward, higher and higher, the square became miniscule, like a black dot in the white room. While in the dream his mind tried to figure out what the square was and what it was trying to tell him. Then suddenly, he was jolted awake by the sense that he was falling.

When he woke he was uncovered on his bed and cold. As he became more conscious, he looked around his room. It was cold and smelled damp and musty. All things seemed to be in order, but he was uncovered. Then, as he thought to make the motion to pull up his covers a shadow from above his head caught the corner of his eyes and he froze, knowing he wasn't alone. There were two figures standing behind his headboard, which seemed impossible. The headboard was pushed all the way up against the wall and yet, there they stood. *Who were they, and what did they want,* he thought. He froze in terror not knowing what to do. Without moving a muscle, he was locked in a position of looking at them as they looked down at him. Their heads were hanging over the bed while staring at him. He was terrified and very cold, but the horror of not knowing what would happen if he moved, caused him to freeze. He fought to stay awake, but in exhaustion and fear, he was not able to keep his eyes open any longer. The two strangers just looked intently at him without moving or blinking. In the morning when he woke up, he jumped up to see that they were gone. He sighed in relief that nothing had happened to him. His room was untouched, no damage and nothing missing. His body and clothing were the same and he was unharmed. Happy that he had survived the night, he still did not understand what had happened.

He ran out of the room quickly yelling, "Mother," as he barreled down the hallway. "Someone was in my room. Someone was in my room."

His mother was sitting at the table drinking coffee and reading the paper when she was startled. "WHAT?" She jumped from her chair and ran with Satya into his room to check out what he was saying.

The Great Gathering of Gods Soul

"What do you mean someone was in your room?" she said with a crease between her brows, expecting an explanation.

Satya replied, "There were two of them, Mother. Last night when I woke up they were standing behind my headboard looking at me. All night they looked at me and didn't move."

His mother looked at the headboard and shrugged it off as a young child's nightmare.

"Oh, you were just imagining that. It isn't possible, Satya. The headboard is pushed all the way up against the wall. People cannot fit behind that. You see," she said as she tried to push her fingers between them and couldn't.

Satya looked at it and although he knew what he saw was real he pretended to agree. Confused, he decided to accept his mother's explanation because it was true, no person could fit behind that headboard. But he saw them-- he knew he did. So instead of making more of it to a disbelieving adult, he logged it in his gee-wiz file and carried on, as children do.

Chapter Two

Endurance

As life went on, Satya continued fighting his mother's awfulness and meditating after school. He would have private talks with his father, who gave him lessons in tolerance and hope, to help him go on. As years went by, he focused on school, playing with friends and then would retreat to his tree house when things got bad. Although life was treacherous with his mother, he did the best he could to maintain his joy and hope for life. But her name-calling and abusiveness became stronger with each passing year. Constant thoughts that he was nothing filled his mind because the voice in his head became his mother's. He struggled internally to shut it out, but it was taking over the world of his thoughts. When things would go wrong in his life, it was her voice he heard in his head, confirming that he would never be anything, and that the reason things never worked out for him was because he was a loser just as she said to him many times.

Then one night his mother had a party with some of her work associates. And although Satya found it amazing that she had friends at all, he watched something wondrous happen to her. She was lovely and kind to her guests and she tended to them with such affection. Like an outsider looking in, he watched her as a child watches ants in an anthill. He observed her and saw that she was capable of love and kindness and in a small way, it brought him comfort. Although she could not give comfort or kindness to him, she was able to show a sort of love to others. If there was only a measure of love in her heart then there was still hope for her. But he knew that her road to enlightenment and love might never reach his destination in his lifetime. Perhaps she would never learn to be a good mother to him, but some day she would know that *he* was more than what she destined him to be.

He set the table and helped to make things as she liked them to be. She performed for her guests so sweetly as though she were an artist playing the role of a rich heiress at a ball. Everything had to be perfect. She was in her own world and barely saw that he was there. She was too busy to even be annoyed with him. He had learned to love that space where he did not exist to her, at least then she was not bellowing at him.

She informed her guests that dinner was served and treated him like a servant, she ordered him what to do and how to do it. She took her seat at the head of the table and a radiant glow filled her face. He could see she felt the power of approval sitting in the king's chair. With a presence so soft, Satya brought out the dinner plates of carne mechada, caraotas negras, arroz, and arepas, and then he filled the glasses around the table with ice water. Many bottles of tequila, ice chillers, and Coca-Cola filled the tabletops, and an elaborate dinner was served. She sat him at the other end of the long table so that he would not be close to her but still within her direct vision to make sure he did nothing that would embarrass her.

The couples were polite and civilized. They seemed joyous in their pairs and talked with one another about little things. Some of the couples were holding hands and kissing, while the others had body language that was open and friendly. They spoke of their work and those they worked with. They spoke of the visual beauty of the table and complimented his mother on her lovely home and meal she prepared. Some of the people at the table even made eye contact with him and treated him as a human being worthy of acknowledgement. He felt wonderful basking in the luminosity of recognition, just by being recognized as a living breathing human being worthy of polite conversation.

Then one of the women at the table spoke to him while everyone else ate.

"Satya, you are so well mannered and polite," she said gazing at him with a smile.

He felt a fondness for her and smiled at her. "Thank you."

The Great Gathering of Gods Soul

Then his mother spoke up over the table with her normal disapproving tone.

"Yes, well, you don't live with the little rag," she said, and she snickered with complete joy in his pain and humiliation.

He was fearful that her badgering would continue, and she would go on to humiliate him in front of all her guests. He felt the trepidation building in him like a tsunami, when the same woman at the table spoke up again.

Satya looked at her and suddenly he saw a brilliant orb of light hit her body like a shock wave. Stunned, he froze, and he could not take his eyes off her. There was no reaction from any of the other guests and he quickly realized that no one had observed what he had seen.

The woman beamed with dazzling warmth and said, "I have it on a greater authority that Satya is more than what you see," she said, never taking her eyes off him. She was blond, American and smelled like fresh flowers. Her rhetorical tone needed no approval from the others, not even his mother.

He felt surprised and relieved that someone saved him from his mother's attack but even more, that someone else stood up to his mother and declared that he did indeed have value. He flashed a subtle smile to the woman and was filled with gratitude. She seemed to say *You're Welcome* in return with hers. She looked intently into his eyes as though she were conveying a message to him that he was important. Then there was a twinkle of light that flashed out from her eyes and was absorbed into the area of his heart. The brilliance exuding from her dispersed, and the table conversation slowly returned back to normal.

"Well," his mother said as if to disagree with her guest as she put another bite of food in her mouth and changed the subject.

Although he knew that later there would be hell to pay for what had just occurred he was mesmerized in what he had seen. His mother was no longer his concern at that moment. He had witnessed something that the others had not seen, and he knew it meant something wonderful, but he did not know what. The woman said *she had it on a higher authority that he would be something more than what they could see.* He clung to those words and continued to believe that life could be more than what his mother said it was. He held on to the idea that he could find more people like the nice woman that saw something worthy in him, enough to stand up to his mother for. He wondered whose authority she spoke of. He believed what had happened was divine and he intended to never forget it. He began to believe again that he mattered.

After that night's experience and as time went on, Satya grew from a boy to a young man of seventeen about to graduate from school. He knew that he should think about the future, but how could? Home had gotten worse over the years and his mother had become unbearable as he became independent. He had taken her verbal beatings for so long that he was now exhausted. As he became a reasonable young man, the visible injustice in the world became more apparent to him and he felt bewildered by his life and by the condition of the world he lived in. His mother had become more horrible than ever before and there was never a time when she could be found happy or kind. She had become belligerent and menacing, continuously and when she looked at him, she had disdain and revulsion in her eyes.

Throughout the years, school became more difficult for him to focus on because she was so callous to him all the time. It was hard o focus when he was emotionally hurting all the time. His grades began to fall from perfection, and the heat of her temper turned up even more when she saw he was not succeeding, because it reflected on her. Reading over his grades she exclaimed, "What's wrong with you, you idiot? Why can't you do anything right? You're no good for anything. You're just a thorn in my side."

Satya became numb to her violent tongue although he knew somewhere in his heart it was bleeding. He wondered why she would continue to gash his open wounds, and for what personal gain? She had almost won her battle to destroy him, and it was very apparent that he was suffering, but she would not let up. He became frail, had circles under his eyes and a

The Great Gathering of Gods Soul

blank exterior to her aggression. Inside him, her words slaughtered any hope he had to be happy. Inside he was crying and begging for her to stop but the more she screamed at him, the more numb he became. She hated his look of no expression and many times she would be angered to the point of physical violence. Slamming him against walls or holding his throat to get a reciprocal, violent response. But he would not reply. His lack of reaction made her rage even fiercer.

She had stopped caring for his needs altogether to punish him and had even refused to furnish him with clothes to punish and humiliate him. Yet, he was blessed with the kindness of friends who gave him all he needed, even before his prayers would go out. He wore hand-me-down clothes, and he did not seem to mind--, not the way that other kids were concerned with their stylish appearance.

He never told a soul of the turmoil he suffered but others who knew him understood. His mother's embarrassing behavior and unpredictability caused him to have few visitors. He was alone most of the time and seemed to be waiting for something, perhaps for his life to start. Many times, he thought of running away but never would because although she was a horrible woman, if he left, she would be alone. As much as she caused him pain, he wished no ill will on her and feared she would be distraught. Or perhaps he hoped that she would?

He would sleep and dream of better lives and still over and over again, the same dream of the white room and the square, large and then becoming smaller, and then the feeling of floating occurred. All through the years, the same dream never stopped coming and it became familiar in his dream world, although he could not understand it.

In time, despite his misery and distraction, he was able to finish school. He graduated and began to think of what he would do with his life. Although he was a young man, he continued to go to his private tree house as he did all through his childhood years and meditate. He'd visit with his father in meditation and go to other worlds and places and the more that he did, the more he felt a strong drive to know what God was

28

about. In his home, he lived a godless existence, but he knew God was out there. He believed and had heard of how God brought joy to others. He longed to have such a joy. All through the years he held onto the faith that something better existed. He wondered if it was God.

While others were busy choosing their college, he was consumed with the condition of the world and how, if God were a loving God, he could allow this world to go on so long the way that it was, with so much suffering? He wanted to learn more about God so that he could understand the world that he lived in and perhaps put the pieces of his own life together. He wanted to find the hope and joy in him once again that was buried beneath the myriad of painful thoughts, memories and bruises of his body and soul. He wanted to know there was a reason for all the madness in the world and in his own. Surely the mysteries of the world were locked up in the awareness of God, the one he knew very little about. Now more than ever he felt a calling to God and if he were to have a chance at a happier life, he must know the truths about Him.

At supper with his mother there was little talk at the table. Then one evening his mother engaged him with a question about his future.

"So, what is it that you are going to do with your life, Satya, so that you can bring some money into this house," she said with an unpleasant tone.

He had learned that her questions were often trickery, and she had long ago squashed any and all of the childhood dreams he had ever had. He answered her questions with neither joy nor reproach. No answer ever pleased her, so he only spoke the truth all the time.

"I will seek God, Mother. I need to understand God," he said somberly, while picking at his food without looking up at her. He took a bite and continued to chew his food when suddenly she shouted, "WHAT! Seek God. What kind of freak are you that you would choose as a profession? After I have spent all my life caring for you and providing for you, you repay

The Great Gathering of Gods Soul

me with choosing a profession that will make no money? YOU WILL..." she said demanding, "choose something else because you owe me with your LIFE for all I have done for you, you ungrateful swine."

Unmoved by her statement he looked up at her. "My life is my own mother," he uttered softly and respectfully.

As he said the words to her, something in him shifted and he felt a sense of purpose. He no longer feared her, and she could do no further damage to him than she had already done by emotionally and verbally abusing him all his life. There was nothing left to fear because the inevitable had become his entire life. He felt a certain freedom in knowing that he could give up the battle with his mother to maintain who he was, because he had already survived her viciousness. She had failed to destroy him and there was nothing more she could do to hurt him; it had all been done. He understood that now it was up to him to change his own life. He held out faith that life would somehow provide a reason for why he had to endure such abandonment and torment the way he did. The thought of seeking answers excited him and he was revived with energy and purpose. His faith was stronger now than ever.

In anger, his mother slammed her hands down on the table, and it made a clanking noise from the sudden jolt of the silverware and dishes that lay on the table. In a rage, she lunged at him, grabbing at his throat; the food and glasses fell to the floor. But he was no longer a boy, easy to manipulate and push around. He was a young man and was now twice her strength. As she shrieked like a wild animal he watched her as though he were out of his body and grabbed her hands with only as much pressure needed to restrain her and make her stop. The tables had turned, and her regular ruse was not going to work anymore. She became quiet and he saw that it was she, this time that felt fear and showed it in her eyes.

"You will never do this to me again mother. Never," he said to her and then released her hands. She stood there dumbfounded and silent. He turned to walk back towards his room and somberly said, "You'll hurt yourself," concerned that

The Great Gathering of Gods Soul

in her aged state she would no longer hurt him but do damage to herself. There was no joy to him in what had taken place although it was the first time in his life he had stopped his mother from hurting him. What joy or victory could he feel when his own flesh and blood assailed him? His quest for God grew stronger with each passing moment in that house. He needed to believe there was a reason for his suffering, for it all and he had to find out what that reason was.

Later that night, while in the midst in the midst of sleep, his mother shook him violently until he was awake. With a quick, sleepy glance at the window he could see it was still dark outside. Startled and confused he sat up.

"Get up now," she said as she began to grab his clothes from the floor where he had left them. "Put these on and hurry up."

"Where are we going?" he asked.

"Shut up and just get your clothes on," she said.

She stood outside his door and kept urging him to hurry up. He walked to his door, and he noticed that her face looked different, even scary, as if she were possessed with a demon. Black makeup ran from her eyes and her face was twisted and angry. She was thinking something horrible, and he knew it, but she had never done anything crazy before, so he waited for her to reveal her evil plot.

"Put some things in an overnight bag," she said, laughing under her breath.

He grabbed a few of his things, put them in his old overnight bag, and then she came into his room and dug her nails into his arm, leading him out of his room and down the hall. In the midst of it all, he put up no fight.

"I am done with you," she said. "I have my own life, you know. Before you came and ruined it."

With the familiar feeling of dread at her unpredictability, he didn't say a word. He wanted to lash out at her, but as always the words of anger choked in his throat. As he passed by all the rooms in the house he looked at them as if he would never see them again. No matter what she was doing to him she could no

The Great Gathering of Gods Soul

longer hurt him. There was nothing left in him to smother. He was without any sensation and in his unfeeling state fear did not exist. Fear only existed up to the point where the unexpected had occurred, and it had. She was a horrible woman and even if she planned to kill him, he found it preferable, than to live one more minute in the torment that had become his life.

Once outside, she shoved him in the car, and still he gave her no resistance. He sat in the back seat where she had pushed him and for hours they drove. They drove and drove until the sun came up and went back down again. She made stops twice at convenience stores for food and also for gas along the way. Neither of them said a word. He didn't know where they were going, and he didn't care.

Satya clutched his bag never looking her in the eyes. He no longer felt anything for her or his life. He felt nothing, not even the rage that he had the right to feel. Finally, early in the morning she seemed to know the area she was driving in and the car began to slow down. They were far away from home, and he didn't know where, nor was he told. He did not care to ask because it no longer mattered to him where he was. The outcome was the same; he was with her, and she had dedicated her life to hating him and making his life miserable.

It was cold outside, so she urged him, "PUT YOUR COAT ON. WE'RE ALMOST THERE."

He did as she asked without hesitation. Like a prisoner he did as he was instructed. The car came to an abrupt stop, and she looked in the back of the car where she had made him sit and said, "GET OUT."

With a creased brow he looked at her and asked, "Where are we?" There were no signs of her parking the car or preparing to exit with him.

"You are exactly where you will always be. Nowhere," she said viciously as she looked him up and down. "You will never be anything, Satya, just like your father. YOU ARE A LOSER and I have hated you since you were born. Now get out of my car. This is your life now," and she shoved him out of the car with her hands grabbing and slapping at his back as she forced him out of the back seat.

As he grabbed his bag and jumped out, the car was already rolling when his feet hit the pavement and she sped off screaming, "Go ahead and *Seek God* now." Mocking him, she continued, "See if he wants you." She laughed wickedly as she drove away. Shocked, he watched her car drive off and out of sight. In disbelief he turned around to see where she had left him. He wondered if she had planned it out in her head a million times because she went to great lengths to drive him out of Manzanillo and to this specific location. She could no longer control him, and his life was no longer hers to make miserable and she had no other use for him.

As he turned around he looked up to see a huge building and the silhouette of a cross in the silver sky just as the sun broke through the clouds. Only this time it was different. He felt free of her. His reaction was a mixture of joy and panic. He felt that he had been set free by his captor but felt the panic of the unknown. Although he was now homeless and in an all-together different predicament, all he felt was liberation. He was free of the cancer that had been eating away at his life. A part of his heart that had been closed for so long, rejoiced inside. But he reserved his folly because life had never been that easy. It was too soon to celebrate; after all, he had no idea what his life would be like now. But even that thought excited him because he could decide for himself who he would now become and what would become of his own life.

He could learn and grow without her constant badgering. She had tried so hard to break his spirit and never could. His father had the same light and she resented him too. Then the words of his father came into his mind. "Love her anyway, Son, she does not know what she is doing."

Standing outside, peace came over him and he decided to aspire to the highest honor of being nothing, nobody, because in the nothingness he was free. But it was not all right to be called a nothing the way his mother shouted, because he had value. With the years of his meditations in the other world with his father, he was grounded in love. His father had taught him well, even in death, and that meant more than anything to him in his physical world.

He could not go back to that house. He could never return. He could not risk that life again. He made up his mind then and there and it was settled. He had a choice to make, and he made it without hesitation. His life would begin from that day forward and he would become what *he* wanted to be, anything he decided.

He glanced sharply at the building where his mother had dumped him. It was a Catholic church. The sign at the entrance read, *St. Joseph's Church,* and he laughed to himself. She had dropped him at a church to ease her own guilt. She had abandoned her own child in front of a church so that she could feel that she had left him in a holy place. It was comical to him that in all her thoughts it was always about her, never for his sake or that of others.

He sat on the steps that led to the huge church doors, and many other thoughts came to mind. He wondered who he would be as a person now. He knew he would be the opposite of her. She had been selfish, so he would be selfless. Although he was sad, he knew now that his life would have a purpose. He would have to choose a path for his life--a path that would surely lead him to some sort of happiness or salvation. He thought that maybe he could help others who had been through painful lives as he had. He wanted to show love to those who were loveless, like he had been.

His heart felt warm and as if it were growing and opening. It was physically painful to open up his heart again to the idea of love and hope, but, he wanted to live a good life, and one without risk was surely no life at all.

Even though he was hurt, he said a grateful thank you to his vile mother because with all the betrayal and trauma she had caused, he now chose a path of resistance which she forced in front of his face through her bitterness. If it were not for her he would have played like all the other children, without any awareness to the reality of the world. But now he was destined

34

for so much more because he knew he must do something to help those who suffer. He wanted to be there for others because no one had been there for him.

He wondered if it was part of his destiny all along, all the pain and strife. He wondered if he was being prepared for something much larger. He felt equipped to help save the world for some mysterious reason. Now, with all his thoughts free to bubble forth, he looked up to the heavens and appreciated the sky, the architecture of the building and everything around him. His hopeful thoughts added color to his world that had been in darkness for so long.

He walked up the steps and decided to enter the church. When he entered through the doors of the church, he was struck by the awesomeness of silence and the sense of holiness. The luminance of the room shined from the flickering lights of the candles, candles that were lit in the hopes that prayers would be heard. He walked toward them and sat in front of the large table that cradled the lights of hope. He sat on the pew, dropped his bag down and sat in silence. His mind was somewhere deep in thought as if his soul were deciding whether it would continue to have faith or give up. The euphoria of his new found freedom began to wear off and the emotional turmoil began to take hold.

He stood and walked to the candles and lit one for himself. He lit a candle for faith. His spirit was not destroyed in totality and his will was still intact. Although it appeared he had nothing to be hopeful for, he still had faith, and he hoped that was enough to create a new world. He decided to pray for his survival and for his sad condition.

"Dear God," he prayed. "Please see to it that my mother gets home safe, and if it isn't too much trouble, could you please help me? I don't know what to do right now." He remained kneeling another moment before he got up and walked back to the pew feeling the exhaustion begin to creep up on him. He looked around and still there was no one in the church that he could see. Tired and drained, he positioned himself to fit on the pew and used his bag as a pillow to lay down on and then closed his eyes. But as he did, thoughts of his father came to mind, and he felt very sad. He loved his father very much and it seemed as though the world was overwhelmingly cruel and unfair. The way life made him grow up as he did, losing his only loving parent so young. He longed for his father to be there to make things all right again. Life seemed so cold, and he wished he were like all the other kids his age who seemed to go through life not noticing the suffering of others. He wished for the blindness others seemed to have that he didn't. He wondered why he had to notice and feel for the suffering of others and hurt so much over it, while others lived in the bliss of their ignorance? But his will was to survive, so there was nothing else to do but rest for now and decide later what he would do next. He felt safe in the church, and it was the first time that he could remember feeling that way since his father died. Maybe he felt safe because he knew that his mother was not coming in at any moment to try and destroy him?

He wondered about her and whom she would torture now? Surely, she was driving home reveling in her plot. But it was all too much to think about. His eyes became heavier than he could withstand and caring little for outward appearances, he fell asleep on the church pew. He left the world of unkind thoughts and followed the glow of the candles that led him to a better place in his mind. A world far better than the one he had known. With eyes like stones, he quickly fell into a deep slumber.

His mind's eye awoke, and he was standing on a rock in the middle of a lake. The mountains glistened with morning dew in the rising sun surrounding the lake. The sky was warm and had the radiance of pink and orange mixed together in perfect symmetry. The mountains silhouetted the beauty of the sky, and he was transformed with the feeling of safety and peace. The water made a slight, soft sound from the rippling water. The hilly landscape was bursting with flowers and the morning bloom bubbled forth an aroma from the life of the earth. Satya stood on the rock in the middle of the lake and felt the delight of the moment's perfect tranquility, as he twirled atop the rock in glee as children do in play. Raising his hands to the sky he experienced an acceptance and softness he had never known with the universe, and it was good.

In the distance, a tall dark man with long dark hair appeared on the water and walked toward him. As the man came closer with each passing step, he became clearer, and Satya was able to make out the whiteness of the man's clothing and his brown wavy hair. The man seemed familiar, but he couldn't place him. His clothes were tattered and worn but still there was regality to the man, with a seeming purpose to every step he took toward Satya.

"Who are you?" Satya asked aloud from the rock.

The man ceased walking on the water and replied, "Who are you? The time has come to remember." Then he turned and began to walk away. The man was close enough to speak and be heard, but still Satya could not make out his face with clarity.

"WAIT! Who are you?" Satya yelled out. But the man gave no reply. He just continued to walk away and as he got further away he began to rise off the water walking upward and into the sky, which swallowed him up into the sensuous glow of warmth and love. The scene was more beautiful than he had ever seen and more peaceful than he could have ever imagined. In amazement, Satya knelt down on the rock and stared up into the sky where the mysterious stranger had disappeared. His eyes wandered back to the slight ripples on the water, and he saw the tepid glow of the sky reflecting on the water. He smiled and took a deep breath of complete serenity. He smiled pleasantly to himself and exhaled, "Ahhhhh." Then suddenly, he felt a shake of his limbs.

Chapter Three

Transition

"Wake up, son," the woman said, lightly touching his arm. Plucked out of the warmth of his dream, he was startled awake. His body jolted up from its peaceful sleep on the pew. He clutched his bag and with his eyes wide open he stared at the woman who woke him while saying nothing. She had auburn hair that looked silky soft while bathed in the light of the candles. Her skin was light golden brown, and her small-featured face expression was soft and loving. She looked exotic and was dressed in the customary garb of India. She was petite and much smaller than he.

"Don't be frightened," she said and smiled while looking him in his eyes. There was kindness in her smile and her voice was melodic. She spoke with a loving tone that he was not used to. She was motherly in the way that he had seen other mothers' affections toward their children. He felt comfortable in her presence.

"You're in a safe place, young man," she said reassuring him and touching his hand with a motherly touch.

Still waking from his dream and being thrust back into the reality of his unkind world, he knew that the next words from her mouth would be a question that he would have to answer. How would he answer a question to why he was there in his sorry state? Suddenly he missed his father, the tree house, their secret meetings and the peace that he had from his dream that was suddenly gone.

"I'm Ke'ren. Do you have a name?" she asked with a playful smile.

"Satya," he replied quietly as he hugged his bag a little tighter.

Her face beamed with a happy glow as if she knew something she had not yet shared. He could not even muster up a facial expression because he felt no inspiration. Looking at the woman, it seemed to him that she could read the pain in his eyes.

"Why are you sleeping on this pew?" she asked with concern. But Satya did not reply. How could he answer such a small question that had such a big answer? He didn't know where to start and so he said nothing. The question only flustered and tired him more.

"Where are you from young man?" she asked, abandoning her first inquiry.

"Manzanillo," he whispered in a downtrodden voice.

"Ah, Mexico," she said with a smile. "And now you are here with me in Costa Rica? I suppose you can tell me some other time about how you got here," she said. "I am in no hurry," and she smiled at him again coyly. "So, you have nowhere to go then do you?" she asked.

"No," he said with exhaustion, too tired to even cry for his sorrow.

"I don't believe in accidents you know. I was drawn here," she said with a knowing wink.

Curious, he did not take his eyes off her. She was his mother's age but very different than the mother he knew. She emoted warmth that his mother did not have. She was soft and attentive.

"There are no mistakes," she replied. "There is only what you do and what you do not do. If you follow the signs you will know what is right," she said with faith. She knelt in front of him in the pew and looked around. "This place is so beautiful, isn't it?" She said as she looked up at the cathedral ceiling to see the pictures of the saints and angels floating in the sky.

"I'm not a Catholic woman but I come here sometimes because it is a place to escape from the world. It has been in histories past, a place to hide in times of trouble. Are you in trouble?" she asked, looking him in the eyes. Her tone was non-judgmental and that of one who sincerely wanted to help.

He could not control his reaction to the question. The tears began to flow down his face but there was no sound. He

39

had trained himself well to not make a sound and it made his tears even sadder to see.

"Yes, that's what I thought," she said.

She stood up from her kneeling position before him and sat on the pew next to him and stared at the candles. "You know, I do believe that we learn the most in life through the experiences that are the most painful," she said, and she took a deep breath as if she understood pain herself. "If things were always good, then we would not appreciate the special times when they come. I know that it doesn't sound very comforting now," she said smiling at him, "but as you grow older, if you are wise, you will learn to accept those hardships as if they were your personal teachers that came into your life, for a short time, to teach you something. If you choose to learn from life instead of becoming bitter, as so many people choose to do, then the long train of troubles will subside. But you must go through it to get to it. There is no answer to *why* things are. They just are," she said.

Satya looked at her and felt the same warmth that his father had generated the night that they had talked in depth about his mother and why he should show compassion to her and to the world. This woman was sincere, and he could feel her goodness in the energy that surrounded her.

She continued, "I choose to believe that if I accept all life's hardships up front then perhaps I can get them all out of the way for the most part," she said, smiling. "Then maybe I will only have an occasional road bump but nothing devastating. At least that is what I hope for. Anyway, you can't stay here. Although it is a church it isn't a place for a young man to live. Unless, of course, you are petitioning to be a priest?" she asked jocularly. Satya shook his head no. "Life is full of signs if you are paying attention," she said looking deep in his eyes. "Like me. I paid attention this morning and instead of going directly to the market I came in here first."

Intrigued by her philosophy on life he continued to listen intently.

"I will leave now and wait outside on the steps for a few minutes. If you read your own signs and those signs lead you out of this church, then I will be waiting. I am staying at the Hotel Santo for just a few more days, my mother as well. We own the mansion, and we visit from time to time. It belonged to my father. We live in India and are going back in a few days. We teach and live at a school out there. Mother will be delighted to see you. Just this morning she stopped what she was doing and said, 'A visitor is coming.' I think you will like her."

He found her comment fascinating and being that she had not mentioned her father, he deduced that perhaps she had also lost her father. Maybe that was why he felt she understood his feeling of being alone and the pain it brings. She touched his arm, smiled politely, rose from the pew and walked outside the church. The sunlight from outside entered the church the moment that she opened the door as if to bring new life to him, and as she did, the smell of the flowers entered the church. He stood and wondered if the smell of the flowers could be a sign about which she was talking. He was intrigued with what her mother said about a visitor coming. Did she know something of his future that seemed so uncertain to him? He couldn't be sure, but he knew he would need to find out more about reading the signs that Ke'ren spoke of, and so he decided to walk towards the door and meet her outside.

He was filled with a different fear than he had ever felt before. Although he did not have to worry about his mother attacking him or screaming now, there was the threat of trusting a stranger and opening up. It was something he had not done for a long time and was leery to trust anyone again. But when he saw her face he felt that it was the right thing to do. He had nothing to lose, and sitting in the church would only bring more strangers and perhaps they would not all be as nice as her?

He grabbed his bag and exited the church, and she was there to greet him as she said she would be. She through her shawl over her shoulder and when he reached her, they walked together up the street saying nothing at first. He felt happy and relieved by her pleasantness. He began to think that maybe life

41

had more to offer than what he had known? The thought brought him a sudden surge of adventure and hopefulness and he appreciated the moment, and he appreciated her.

"Where is your mother and father?" she asked casually. "Have you run away?"

"No," he answered. Although it was hard to begin, he told her the story of the earlier scene starting at his home and leading all the way up to the church. He spoke of his mother and proceeded to share the story of his life and the hardships he faced with her cruelty. Ke'ren's face showed a look of sadness at the events that had led up to his arrival at the church.

"I am sorry that happened to you, Satya," she said. "You must come with us back home and stay with us as long as you like. I will do all I can to help you. No child should endure such betrayal, but I can see from the look in your eyes that all these years you have refused to let her break your spirit. I see the familiar glare of a fighter in your eyes. Never lose that, Satya. It is the stare of determination, and you will need it throughout life."

Satya looked at her as they walked through the market doing her shopping. As they talked he listened and absorbed her every word and friendly glance. It was soothing to his soul to be treated with kindness. So, he took all she had to offer him, and she didn't seem to mind.

"Never let anyone tell you what you can be or what you can do, Satya. Seeking approval is a very dangerous game. Believe within yourself who you are. No one else defines who you are, but you. That is truth, you know? It is what you believe it is, whatever that may be. So, make it something wonderful."

He began to understand that she was saying that if he believed something to be true, he was, in essence, creating a world for himself. Whether anyone agreed with it or not, he had the right to believe what he wanted to believe in. He felt enlightened by the thought and her words gave him dignity and hope. He felt encouraged in her presence and more loved by her in the short time he had known her than he had felt his whole life by his mother. He felt happy, but even still, there was the dull ache for the love he knew he had been lost for so long. Every child longed for the love of its mother, and nothing could fill that void.

In his silence, she instinctively said, "In time my dear. It will pass."

He smiled at her in gratitude for what she said to comfort him. They began to walk through the many trees that were lining the streets on the way to her destination. "Do you know what these trees are?" she asked him.

"No, I don't," he said looking at her.

"These trees are native to Costa Rica. They are called Guanacaste. This too is an Omen, Satya," she said to him looking deep into his eyes as a breeze passed by them. "These sacred trees represent renewal of one's faith and the power of free choice, given to you by God," she said and continued walking. He took into his heart the words she had said and logged them into his memory thinking of his own faith and free will.

They reached the Hotel Santo and walked passed the beautiful, grand lobby with marble floors and imported draperies leading to her room. He smelled the sweet aroma of the flowers again that he had smelled in the church. He looked to see where it was coming from but there was nothing around. He enjoyed the fragrance but said nothing of it.

"I know, it smells lovely, doesn't it? It's mother's doing, she can meditate and throw a scent anywhere and it lingers for days. It's how I know when she is calling for me," Ke'ren said.

Can that be true? He thought to himself as he listened and smiled at her as they entered the room. He did not feel brave enough to ask questions, in regard to her interesting thought.

She was mystical, and although he had never met anyone like her before, who said the things she was saying, he felt an ease around her that was almost familiar. "I can't wait for you to meet her," Ke'ren said about her mother.

As he entered the room, he saw that it was a majestic French Victorian villa, yet had an Indian flare, no doubt from their native influence. There were spiritual symbols all over the rooms that he had never been exposed to before. Some he recognized from books and magazines that he had read when he was trying to escape the reality of his childhood world. The statues everywhere were most assuredly what they had brought with them from their homeland because they did not seem to match the design of the rooms. Ruby-colored sheer flowing drapes hung over each doorway entering into the next room and it was dreamy to look at. He felt as if he was passing through someone else's dream. He seemed to be in another dimension, slowing time itself in order to absorb all that his eyes could take in.

"Come meet my mother, Satya. You will love her, and she you," Ke'ren said as she looked back and smiled at him. She pushed back the drapes, and they entered the room.

"Yes, you're right," Ke'ren's mother said with her back to them, sitting in an elegant chair. Then turning around to see Satya's face as he entered, she said, "It is *my* dream you are walking through," and she smiled at him.

"How did you know what..."

"Because you are in my world now, my dear," she said standing up and coming towards him. She then reached for both his hands to gently hold them out to her. "In my world, I know what I choose to know, and hear all that I want to hear. Yours is the voice that will save," she said.

"Mother, this is Satya," Ke'ren said introducing him.

Satya, taking the old woman for somewhat of an eccentric, smiled at her and made no comment. Tilting her head and giving him a discerning look, she said, "Eccentric, huh," and laughed. As Satya's eyes bulged she put her arm over his shoulder and walked him toward the sitting area so that they might have tea and talk. He was momentarily rattled yet humbled by her keen ability to see and hear him internally.

"Your journey is just beginning, Satya. There is much to remember and learn so we will not waste any time." And she showed him to a chair to sit in.

He felt their generous hospitality and the villa was so cheerful, peaceful and alive with rich colorful expressions of happiness and the aroma of chandan in the air.

44

"I knew you would come," the old woman said softly and passed him a cup of tea. "I honor and acknowledge the god in you, dear one," she said raising her tea cup to him and taking a sip.

. "My name is Asha. As you can see I am the Indian half of my lovely daughter. Her father passed away a few years ago and I suppose someday soon I will join him. But there is work to do first," she said happily.

The sound of Ke'ren singing in the background was blissful as though she were serenading them while occupied with her own busy work.

"This mansion had been in her father's family for many generations and so when we travel and visit, we stay here, check on the hotel and visit family. In time Ke'ren will inherit this place," she said looking around the ceilings and admiring the structures and tapestries. "Knowing her, she will turn this place into a school for children. She is so generous, my daughter," she said thoughtfully of her daughter as her eyes beamed with love for her flesh and blood.

"Yes," Satya replied. "She also spoke of India and teaching there. What is it that you teach?" he asked, deciding to come out of his shell.

She smiled at the question. "We help awaken the spirit of those who wish to wake from their sleep walk through life. Awareness is not something learned but known all along in the spirit and soul of a person. Life in the body teaches us to sleep, the reawakening of awareness is to rejuvenate all that we already know but have forgotten."

Intrigued, he beckoned her to continue by nodding his head and listening intently.

"We have come into life *all knowing,* Satya. But through the world's domestication, we are trained to numb our senses to the spiritual world and hence, forget who we really are. We come into this physical world knowing all that we need to know, lose it through the physical domestication process of life and then, as adults, we spend the rest of our lives searching for what we came into this life with, but lost," she said explaining the complexity of a simple truth. "That very loss is the reason we feel empty and try to fill it with anything, even empty pursuits. Emptiness is just the symptom of the self we have forgotten and long to return. Our memories have been covered, but not erased," she said calmly. "But it is not the mind we need to remember. Intellect is the mind of the body. The mind of the soul can forget nothing, the imprint is timeless, transcendental, and it has only become silent. But it retains all the wisdom of all the lives we have ever had, and it can recall them, if one seeks to awaken them," she said.

"Is this what you teach at your school?" he asked with haste.

"Yes, among many other things," she answered. "So, you will come then?"

"I haven't anywhere to go, but I haven't any money either," he said believing that the lack of money made him unworthy for the trip.

Asha laughed out loud with a pleasant giggle.

"Oh, silly young man, look around, we are rich," she said laughing and tossing up her hands. What do we need with your money? Money is just an obstacle and we have already removed that barrier for you. So, it seems you are free to roam in our world and learn again who you are. It is written, Satya, it was no mistake that Ke'ren found you. If you stay for a time, you will read the signs yourself," she said and then sipped her tea.

Satya looked at her and smiled. He was in a new world, and it was fascinating and almost overwhelming. It was too soon for him to begin his new life so quickly. He had hardly absorbed what had happened that morning and the thoughts of his father swam in his mind. He would never see the tree house again and he wished he could be there to make him feel safe again. He was tired and emotionally drained, even in the face of promise. His heart still sprouted weeds of lament for his silent pain and flashes of bitterness and anger at his mother for being so cruel. There was a black rose in the garden of his soul.

"So, I suppose sooner or later I will hear the story of what happened to you, but you must know that I have been given a gift of sight and knew that you were coming, son."

"What do you mean?" Satya said politely.

"I have only ever had one child, my daughter Ke'ren. After she was born I was not able to have more. But I had a vision long ago when I was younger, that I would have a son. He would not be born flesh of my flesh and I was told that I would hold spiritual keys of truth, to which I would pass on to him before he began his long journey of life-giving salvation."

Satya creased his brow in thought trying to understand what was going on, but never once did he doubt her words. There was sincerity to her words and a sense of honor and urgency. The women's character could tell no lies nor do any harm; it was obvious to him. He understood that without question, although he had never been around people quite like these women before.

"Now, tell me all about your life. I want to know everything," she said, settling into her chair and looking him in the eyes.

Ke'ren entered the room hearing what her mother had just asked him and said, "Momma, why don't we let Satya rest a bit before we get into that. He has had a rough few days."

"Oh yes, dear. You are right," Asha said, looking at Ke'ren and then him. "I'm sorry, Satya, I was only thinking of myself, I am so excited to talk with you. I have been in this room all morning singing and meditating and haven't thought about what you must have been through today. Although I do know that it was difficult, sweetheart. Forgive me," she asked him and touched his hand.

"Of course," Satya said in his soft-spoken and polite manner.

He sat back on the recliner and relaxed his body in it and the chair seemed to swallow him up. He felt as though he disappeared into the chair, and it felt good to disappear. He was hurting in his heart, and as much as he wanted to forget, he wanted to remember his life. In the process of letting down his

47

guard with the women and finally relaxing, all the sadness of his life visited him, and he felt as though he wanted to die. He wondered about his mother and how someone could be so cruel to him all his life? But as quickly as the thought came, he buried it again and returned to his survival instinct that he had known all his life.

"Dear One," Ke'ren said to Satya. "You will have to call home to let her know you are all right."

Asha quickly put her teacup down in disagreement. Her facial expression became cross, and she spoke to Ke'ren in her native tongue.

"Momma, it has to be done. Have faith in your vision," she said looking into her mother's eyes for understanding. He must do it to know that he tried. He must do it or he will have regret and it will hinder his growth." Satya just looked at them as they decided his fate.

He felt fear in having to call her. What if his mother changed her mind and wanted him to come back? He didn't want to go back. He would rather live on the streets than go back. The streets were safer than living with her. But he knew Ke'ren was right. He was his mother's son, and he didn't want the women to get in any trouble for housing him. *Maybe she had regret for what she had done? Maybe there was some remorse, she had never gone this far before,* he thought with dread but also hopefulness.

With the women still in a disagreement over the right thing to do, Satya announced," I will do it." and climbed out of the recliner. The women became silent and looked at each other as he got up and went to the phone that he had passed earlier on the way in. Standing before the phone he picked it up and said quoting Ke'ren, "There are no mistakes. There is what you do and what you don't do. There is no right thing to do."

The women went quickly to him to see what he would say and what would happen next. He dialed the number and waited. He held the phone to his ear for a few seconds and then hung the phone up slowly as his head dropped to his chest and he began to cry like a baby.

48

"What happened, son?" Asha asked. He looked up at her with swollen eyes and red with tears.

"It was disconnected," he said. "She made sure I couldn't come back." His last fairytale hope for a mother's love was destroyed. He returned to the room they had been having tea in and sat back down in the recliner. The women followed behind him closely, and Asha sat in the chair next to his and Ke'ren sat in front of him on the floor, at his feet. With compassion, both women tended to his sadness with their silent, comforting presence. Asha moved her head to his lowly position and caught his eye as he looked up at her. She touched his hand that was in his lap and said, "It was meant to be, child. New birth is always preceded by pain." Her eyes filled with tears for his pain and Ke'ren began to cry for the child in him who had suffered so. In a silent gathering, they mourned his old life that was passing and cried together for an ending that was both hurtful and joyous.

Chapter Four

Honor

Later that evening they showed him to his room that was across from Ke'ren's room and before Asha's. They approached a grand door that was different than the other doors. When they opened it, to his surprise, it was fit for a king. The walls were gold, and there were many pillows atop the bed in deep, rich colors of ruby red, gold and purple. Beads hung over the oversized wooden closet doors and entryways. In the corner there was an oversized antique dressing table.

He entered the room and stood in amazement with the room and all its beauty and colors. He could not believe the lush treatment he was receiving from two mere strangers, but he accepted their kindness gracefully. He turned to the women to look at them and they smiled at him and began to shut the door.

"We were expecting you," Asha explained with a bright smile as she bowed her head to him and closed the door. Neither of the women ever entered his room.

He was intrigued by their behavior. There was something enchanting about the women and not of this world. They were mystical and divine, operating on a higher plane that he had not witnessed before. The women were innately aware of his needs and seemed to understand without words what he had been through and that it all led to a greater purpose. He found their ways inspiring and to be a source of divine influence.

The women had known of his arrival and had prepared for clothes to be in his room. There were fresh white linen pants and a matching long sleeve shirt that flowed like all the drapery and tapestry in the villa. He slipped it on and felt as though he was putting on new skin. He felt so much gratitude for the most generous women he had ever known. No one had given him anything for him for longer than he could remember and here it was that two women he had never met before bestowed such a gift on him.

He felt emotional and tired with his eyes and body feeling heavy like a barrel of rocks. The emotional turbulence from the recollections of his life had drained him of every last drop of energy. He lit the tea light candle by the bed and turned out the light. He climbed up on the bed and pulled the pillows away enough for him to settle in and turned to face the light of the moon. It was shining in from the window outside, a full moon so large that it seemed close enough to touch. He thought of his life and of his life's pain through the years. There was an aching in his belly from all the memories swimming in his soul until he reached the point of despair. He could not forget the feeling of being forsaken by his mother and how much that hurt. While he lay there in bed, he wondered for many hours, trying to understand how a mother could find joy in destroying the flesh of her flesh. Finally, sleep came to his rescue.

He woke the next day to the rising sun and still the women's kindness continued to him. They showered him with food, drink, clothes, and all the necessities of life that he had been denied his whole life. Most importantly, they gave him dignity and value by showing him love, compassion and respect. Days passed in the same manner and then the women began to prepare for their return to India. They had treated him so well and he was thankful to them, never taking their hospitality for granted. He never said another word about his mother since the phone call and the women did not push him to speak about it. The inner world of his thoughts, however, was solemn and as much as the women gave him their love unconditionally, he felt alone and sad beneath the surface. He continually heard his mother's vile words in his head. "You're a loser...you'll never be anything, see if He wants you," and how it translated to him in his heart and mind was, *you are unworthy, you are nothing, you are valueless*. In his thoughts he carried her words and the damaging pain they brought. He could not escape his own mind that tortured him so. Part of his self-image was still wrapped up in being what she said he was. Although he knew it was not true that he was not a loser or valueless, the realization of who he could be had not yet caught up with his freedom from his villain.

Life with the women was easier for him and he knew that the memory of his mother would become faint with each day and passing year. But still, there was rage in him, and it seemed to be growing. He had bottled up all his injuries for years, until he was numb. It was the day before the women were going to leave and still he did not know if he would go with them or not. His indifference was motivated by the negativity and suppression of the feelings he had had for so long. He had no fear of what would become of his life anymore, but he longed for something to make up for the childhood he lost, or someone who would be there for him and not betray him.

He left the hotel and walked the streets in the dark night and felt isolation and anger. He began to think back on the years of observing people and how they would pair up. He watched others getting the affection he longed for and while he was happy for them, it made his longing deeper. There was a feeling that he could see in others, who felt they belonged to the world and the people in it. They were the loved ones of the world. He watched people and how they were consumed with romantic love and seemed impervious and oblivious to the evil of the world. He wondered how they could not see the famine, death, disease and injustice of the world. They seemed unaware of the real world that was happening around them and he longed to be like them. But he could not unlearn what he knew or un-see what his eyes had already beheld. Then as it always happened, he would remember what his father told him, and it always shined a bright light into his dark world of awareness. He remembered his father saying that he was not part of the world and when he accepted that, the longing for it would end.

He thought about God and wondered, *If God were love, then how could he let some live and be wealthy while others die with nothing when abundance is everywhere? How could he let his children starve to death and die of disease, abuse or starvation? How could he allow people to kill each other and have wars? Why would he let some parents struggle and have to work many jobs to feed their young while others who have no families at all are provided for abundantly? How could He, the creator of it all, not tell mankind the purpose to life in order to give them a reason to keep living? He wondered how God could*

52

let him grow up in a household the way that he did and do nothing to help him. If he was love, then why did he just leave him there, abandoning him, he wondered.

As he walked the streets of San Jose, throbbing with anguish, he pondered many questions, but the answers were not there. With blackness in his soul, he turned back towards the Hotel Santo. As he approached closer his attitude toward life spoiled. His anger was boiling and coming to the surface for all he had ever suffered.

As he entered the grand lobby of the Hotel Santo, the host at the reception desk saw him and placed his hand out to deliver a white envelope. "For you, sir," he said. Satya froze, noticing a glisten in his eyes, the same as he had seen before on other mystical situations. Once delivered, the man went back to his business without missing a beat. Satya opened the envelope and to his surprise it was a first class, one-way ticket to India, leaving in the morning. The women made sure that whether he came back to the room or not, there was a road out if he wanted to take it.

He knew the women would be wondering where he had been, but he was lost and absorbed in himself and his past. He was bitter at the pangs of his life and so the anger within his soul bubbled forth. He entered back into the private villa of the women and found them busy packing things into their crates. They stopped at the sight of him and looked at each other. With the shadow of anger cast on his face, Asha looked at him with a confrontational glare.

"Why don't you just say it, boy, and stop holding the river that builds inside?" she said. Ke'ren, standing by her mother's side, nodded her head in agreement and tilted her head to get a better look at his eyes.

"If God is love than how could he allow babies to die with bloated bellies of starvation? How could he destine other children to search for their meals in dumpsters, how could he allow some to die horrible, violent deaths and let others be rich and famous giving them more money than they could ever spend? What did I do so wrong to deserve to be hated and thrown away by my mother? To have my father ripped from my life, to not ever fit in with anyone because I belong nowhere. I have nothing. I am no one, nothing, just as my mother said," he said. Lowering himself to the floor, on his knees, he began to cry.

His feeling of loneliness and fear was so strong, and he was afraid his life would be filled with more of the same. He worried that his life would reflect his mother's anger and he would be destined to become what she said. Although he knew he was a good person filled with love and compassion for others, the small voice in his head came to him always, "You are a loser, and you will never be anything." He heard his mother's words and he saw in his mind's eye, her grisly looks she used to intimidate him. It was there always, especially when he felt low, deepening his torment.

"I just want to die," he said giving up the struggle in his soul to be silent. Sobbing uncontrollably, he felt the heat in his nose and eyes begin to burn from the release of his tears. Then, touched by a hand on his arm, he looked up with his swollen face wet with tears.

It was Ke'ren kneeling down to his level looking into his eyes. "Live," she said in a whisper as she handed him a yellow rose she had taken out of the nearby vase. Her single word 'Live' was so sincere and for the first time, he felt that someone in the universe actually cared about his existence. She cared if he was alive or dead and the look on her face assured him that someone did love him, and it made him sob even more.

Ke'ren held him in a loving embrace, rocking him to quiet his tears and when he seemed to catch his breath, she said, "Let it go so you can be free, Satya. It was not your fault."

Satya looked at her and she handed him a tissue. He nodded with understanding but still it hurt.

"What she did to you was not about you at all but the pain in her own heart, Satya. Don't let her win, sweetheart," Ke'ren said kindly. "Fight the good fight and become what you believe you can be. Because all that matters is what you believe you can do. You control your own destiny, child. It's your world

54

now; perhaps what she did to you was to build the anger in you, to make you decide."

"Decide what?" Satya asked sadly.

"Decide whether you will follow your destiny or become a distant second to who you really are," she said. "Perhaps it was all part of your sacred task?" Satya looked at her confused because he did not understand.

"You must decide who you will be right at this very moment, Satya. Will you fight to become the man you were destined to be, or will you give in to the voice in your head that is not your own? Will you destine yourself for great things or to misery? Only you can decide that" she said and then there was silence. Asha watched and listened but did not say a word.

What she said made perfect sense to him and although the anger was still inside him, it began to fight for his survival, and he felt a second wind come through his body, so he stood up.

"I choose to drown out the voice in my head that says I am nothing." He said as he looked at Ke'ren. Ke'ren smiled at him and then looked at her mother who was beaming because he had made the right decision.

"I choose that no one will tell me who I will or will not be. I decide," he said. "I DECIDE."

Asha walked over to him and kissed his forehead while holding each side of his face. "I knew you were in there," she said referring to his true nature, smiling and then walking off to go to bed.

"Get some rest, Satya. We leave for India tomorrow and it will be a long journey," Ke'ren said as she kissed him goodnight.

Satya watched her walk away down the hall until she disappeared into her room. He moved his hands to his lips, as if in prayer, and felt hopeful and excited about the next day.

He thought how odd life was and how, with a twinkling of an eye, his life had changed. Then, he too laid to rest with that very thought in his mind. He knew the next day would be momentous. It would be the day that he would begin his journey to becoming the man he wanted to be. It was a rite of passage and an example of what someone could do with personal choice.

When morning came the women were not in the villa. So, he dressed quickly as the servants were collecting the women's belongings, loading all their chests full of statues, drapery and clothing. Once dressed, he calmly walked out of the room, through the grand lobby to the outside of the hotel as his feet were guiding him. When he was outside, he saw that there was a black limousine waiting. As he walked slowly to it, the luxurious limousine door opened as if by magic. He felt the pull of surrender to enter inside and when he looked deeper into the car he saw the women smiling, awaiting him inside.

He got into the limo without hesitation and the limo driver asked, "To the airport, sir?" Satya looked at the women who were smiling at him excitedly and he responded with a yes. They were taken from the Hotel Santo to the San Jose airport. Once inside, he gave the attendant his boarding pass, entered the plane, sat, buckled up and flew out of Costa Rica. He felt no remorse for leaving to such a faraway place; he only felt the surrealism of the moment. He cherished it, knowing that his life would be forever changed from that moment on. He knew that he could no longer be hurt by the past because it was just that, in the past, and he had chosen to forgive and move on. Most importantly, he would find the answers to life that he so earnestly sought after. Life was full of promise for him now, and it could get no worse than where his life had already been, so he felt no fear, for anything. He felt free and limitless for the first time in his life.

Asha carried on board with her a worn and tattered black leather bag. It looked to him like an old-fashioned bag that doctors used to carry when they still made house calls, only it was much larger. He wondered what was so important that she needed to carry it on board with her as nothing else came on board. The women took their seats behind him and left him in the privacy and comfort of first class, with an open seat next to him to spread out. He sat excitedly and began to watch others, intrigued by the experience, as it was his first time he had flown anywhere.

After a while, the boredom began to set in. Asha took the seat next to him for a moment and, with a knowing glance, opened her bag atop her lap. It was filled with books, among other female things that were important to her. She pulled out three books and placed them on his lap.

"Start with these young man and mark this as the day of your awakening. You now know that one path leads to another," she said and watched for his reaction. He picked up the books and looked at them, three of the most well-known books of the world's religions and philosophies. He began to read and did so the entire trip, fascinated by the wisdom.

The entire trip had passed while he read and eventually they landed in India. He knew they all would soon be ushered off the plane to the school that the women taught in. As he exited the plane the women's face beamed, awaiting his reaction to their homeland. The setting of India, its rich colors, liveliness, and the smell of distant foods mixed with the dirt and soil between his feet was priceless and mesmerizing to him. The enormous crowds of people overwhelmed him. Some were waiting to get on the planes, some were waiting for loved ones, and the merchants were everywhere trying to sell them products. Electric and foot-pedaled rickshaws passed on the roads continuously giving people rides to and fro in the city. He felt radiant and enlightened just by being alive and being on life's journey. He sensed a sacredness and familiarity for India although he had never been there before. Strangely, he felt as if he were returning home, instead of arriving for the first time. He was alive with anticipation to learn and became lost in the reverie.

At the gate he noticed two men holding signs saying, *Ashram House*. The drivers had come to retrieve them and to take them to the place called *Ashram House* were the women lived and taught. He had asked Asha on the drive there about the Ashram

House and she expounded. It was a very old mansion that had been owned by a millionaire and sold many times over before Asha purchased it to further her philanthropy work. The house had a feeling of simple elegance, but the dark wood was carved so precisely that it was not a house but a work of art. In the entrance was a marble statue of a saint named Baba adorned in his robe with his arms stretched out as if to embrace the world from its suffering. The plaque beneath Baba's statue read, "*God manifests in us all.*"

On the journey home, they shared the roads with parades of bicyclists, sputtering motorcycles, rickshaws, cows everywhere, tinseled trucks, camel carts and an occasional goat. There were so many people, sights and markets that the chaos of the busy, overcrowded city was breathtaking. When they arrived at the home, the servants collected their bags and chests full of all their belongings. Asha walked down a hallway that was adorned with dark wood, with garnet-colored carpeting and velvet covered walls. Statues of Shakti, Shiva, Ganesh, Parvati, Krishna and many more adorned the hallways as if they were greeting her return home. As Asha disappeared from sight down the mystical looking hallway, Ke'ren looked at Satya and said, "We will go this way," and she took him up the staircase carved out of what seemed to be a single oak tree. The house's beauty and the tapestries that hung everywhere blowing in the wind entranced him. He understood that the women hung them in the hotel in an effort to replicate the look and feel of their home. He noticed while still in his daze that the home had no windows or doors. Only entryways adorned with silk in the richest and most beautiful colors he had ever seen. Red, purple, fuchsia and green and others, all mixed together. As he watched the wind blowing through the home, moving the silk in its current, he felt the profound love of nature touch his soul and he felt safe. He felt connected with the feeling of nature and how it asked nothing of him but gave its love freely. It was a part of God created for all people, no matter how much money they had, no matter who they were or how they were raised. Nature discriminated for no one, and it shared its beauty with all whom would see and feel

58

it. In that moment he felt as though he were in a place that could shelter him from the storm that had been his life.

The servant followed closely behind Ke'ren with her things as she showed Satya to his room. They walked him to the entryway of his room and pulled the flowing drape aside for him to enter. Ke'ren nodded for him to go in.

"Go in and get comfortable. You will find clothing in the wardrobe closet," she said. "It has been prepared for you already. Do as you wish, and we will call for you when it is time to eat. You will feel tired soon from the time difference and when you do, give in to it," she said to him with a smile.

"Okay," he said, returning the smile, and turned to look at his room. It was so beautiful. Everything was made of the same dark wood with elaborate circular carvings, life-sized statues of deities that were breathtaking and felt holy. He walked to the wardrobe closet to see that they had provided him with beautiful linen suites, much like the others the women had bestowed upon him before but in every color. Solid colors like tapestries, purple, red, tangerine, black and white. All in his size with accompanying cotton slippers to match every outfit.

He could hear the sound of a tranquil running fountain outside his room, and birds chirping. He moved aside the tapestry to glance out and saw the small birds bathing in the water. He turned around to look at his room and took a moment to smell the spicy scent of incense, which ran throughout the house. He heard the chime of the tiny bells that were attached to some of the curtains, as they blew in the wind.

Satya turned his attention to the clothes and saw that the pants flowed, and the shirtsleeves hung long. He put his bag down and dressed himself in his new clothing. Looking at himself in the full-length mirror he saw the image of a man. It was himself and he realized that he was changed forever. He stood before his reflection and in seconds saw his transformation from the boy he was to the man he was becoming, marked by his passage to India. It was a glorious transformation, and he was so pleased that he burst out with happy laughter. He was humble, grateful and compassionate. His path to enlightenment had begun and his past was fading to the blackness of yesterday's garden of weeds. He felt there was something new growing in his heart and it was hopeful and full of promise.

Chapter Five

The Divine Within

His studies had begun at the Ashram House and although he was nervous, there was a sense of excitement to learn. His mind was thirsty for knowledge and quenched by his immersion in the water well of awareness. He studied with dedication the teachings of Hinduism and learned about Baba, a man who believed in love and acceptance for all, whose real name was never known. He read the hymns, incantations and rituals from ancient India and was fascinated. He followed the ten great observances of patience, firmness and stability, forgiveness, self-control and contentment, to not steal, conceal or be selfish, to be clean, pure and honest, have control over senses and sexual energy, right knowledge of the scriptures, spiritual knowledge, truth and the importance of the absence of anger.

He learned about the Hindu Trinity of God which was made up of Brahma-- representing creation, Vishnu--representing preservation and Shiva--representing dissolution. The supreme god is the generator of all life, preserver of all life and even the destroyer of all life.

He meditated with Hatha yogins and became quite good at it. He even followed local rituals of posing upside down with his head in a hole all the way up to his torso, wearing a red loincloth. Life to him was exciting and new.

He began to pay homage to the three debts in life: dedicating himself and his life to the service of all mankind, serving society and the poor without expectations, and acknowledging his debt to his ancestors by sending loving energy to his mother and meditating daily with his father.

He studied endlessly and learned Asha and Ke'ren's native languages of Hindi, Urdu and Sanskrit. He learned the industry of India and their export of textiles that were evidenced all over the Ashram house. Their inner world and spiritual kingdom became his. He could understand why the worlds outside their own would want to buy such tapestries. The soft loveliness of the silk was impeccable, and the colors stunned and elevated his mind to a higher realm, simply by looking at them. He learned the currency of a rupee and the value of wheat and rice, which was something they ate daily in their simple life. Daily foods consisted of bread called naan, rice with literally every meal, vegetables mixed with curry, Channa Dal-dried pulses and lentil--similar to yellow split peas only sweeter and smaller, spicy chicken, kebabs and grilled trout.

The women spent endless days and nights faithfully teaching him the Sanatana dharma--the eternal law and order of spirituality and spoke of a soul that could not die. They taught him the pantheon of gods representing the Supreme God. Days turned into weeks, weeks turned into months, months turned into years of being taught the subjects of incarnation, divine deities, Hindu history, and the importance of having compassion and love for others and accepting all people. He was touched beyond anything that he had ever felt before by the concept of understanding mankind's sameness in suffering and in wanting to find peace. The Guru's taught him the Vedas, which were the most sacred of scriptures, and from them he understood that the negative ways that one creates always return to its source. During that time, he took moments to stop and pray for his mother. He began to understand the power of symbols and statues and that they served as a reminder to the people how to be better human beings. And from what he had seen in the world, human beings often needed it.

In the home, on the streets, in the market and on the road, the women inculcated the ways of divinity to him. As he learned their rituals he transitioned from an insecure boy to a man with much love and kindness, and the women became his family-- a family of choice. He finally understood what love was. He read the books that Asha had given him that day on the plane and many others, while he learned the prominent philosophy of India. Yet he knew that there was so much more to be learned in the world. He knew there were others in various parts of the world who had found spirituality and peace while knowing

62

The Great Gathering of Gods Soul

nothing of Hinduism, and the thought only made him want to understand others more.

The women, gurus and swamis from past and present, taught him many things but what he found most effective was to live in the present, and *that teaching* opened his eyes to spiritual ways he had never know before. During that time, he awakened to the wisdom that there existed not only one, but many ways that human beings seek out the favor of God. All faiths were acceptable, and the understanding and peacefulness that it brought about in him also inspired him.

He learned the teachings of Baba and the Ashram House and hoped for utopia that to him could be a reality if the human race became fully aware of its true nature of greatness. He was taught that divinity was all around him always and that he must realize his own divine power. But with all his awareness he was still bothered by a world that did not want to see all that it could be. Injustice, death and suffering continued on unstoppable, and he began to see that the journey of all mankind was like a thread woven into a cloth that ultimately twined humanity together. The progress of the world had changed nothing.

The Ashram house, to him, was a place that was helping mankind further the realization of who they really were. It seemed to him that there were few in the world outside of Ashram that seemed to grasp the greater glory of those teachings. Not even in the most educated of metropolis cities, or worlds far, far away from India. He looked deeper at the life process and how the world trains a child how to become an adult. The world's system of things would spend eighteen years to domesticate a human being to conformity in worldviews that perpetuated fear, deceit, betrayal, materialism and loss of self. At the Ashram house in India, he was taught to recognize the truth of the human spirit. They reawakened in him the understanding that people come into life knowing all that they are but are smothered by the ways of the world and born again into a world of confusion, fear and lies. They are taught they must earn the right to be valued. Then people would spend the rest of their lives trying to regain awareness of who they were born to be.

The Great Gathering of Gods Soul

Life was not a dream but a nightmare to which most were not even aware that they were asleep. He understood that awareness was not something learned; awareness was always present and was the true state of a soul. But people had become lost in their body, instead of remembering they were a limitless spirit. The memory of who they were had been removed by the ways of the world and choked until there was nothing left but surrender and walking with the living dead. The women saw his true nature even when he was not sure.

He began to see how lost he had been in his childhood world. But he reflected how it only took someone to care for him to bring him back from the slumbering underworld. It was the women who cared for him and shook him from his long dead wake up.

The women were his heroes for showing him instead of telling him that he had value or what love really was. Because the women reiterated what his father had told him about his value, he believed he could make a difference in the world and in the lives of others. He wished, not for material goods, but to help all the unloved people of the world. He wanted to help those that were lost or worse, had lost their worth. He wanted to love others so they would know they were not alone or isolated in the cruel world.

There was beauty in the world waiting to be realized. He knew there was. It was evidenced in all the temples that he had traveled to see throughout his training and learning at Ashram. He journeyed to many cave temples, dating back to 578 A.D. There were many cave temples built, all mystical and unique. He had to climb more than forty steps to the first cave made of red sand stone, before he reached the hall of pillars and square-shaped sanctum hollowed in the back wall.

The bottoms of his feet were hot and dirty, and the air was dry in his nostrils. Still, he was happy, not only for seeing the temple, but also for seeing the families of monkeys who played in then. He was amazed at how the temples were built from solid rock, and carved into them, very elaborate rooms and drawings. There was another cave atop a sandstone hill

64

dedicated to Lord Vishnu, who was depicted as a dwarf of awesome dimensions with one foot mastering the earth and the other, the sky.

Going higher was a cave nearly seventy feet wide and on the plinth, Satya could see the carvings of Ganas. The air was becoming thinner, and he was beginning to sweat, still, he moved on. The artistry and sculptural genius was breathtaking. The cave that he found most interesting was that of the only Jain cave that was begun in the sixth century and finished nearly one hundred years later. In it was a fifty-seven-foot-high statue of the saint, Gomateswara. He sat and watched the Jains worship at his huge feet made of rock while they adorned it with flowers, tea and rice offerings. Some even cried at its feet in gratitude, and he felt touched at their display of humility.

The Thousand Pillar Temple, a star-shaped temple with three shrines dedicated to Lord Shiva, Vishnu and Surya, was built on a one-mile platform. There was black basalt Nandi, polished and carved from a single stone. Surrounding the gardens were lingam pillars and he had to laugh because he had never seen before a garden surrounded by statuesque penises. But even through his laughter he knew that they were there as a blessing of fertility to the gardens and to the universe.

The Iskon temple, built for Krishna consciousness, beckoned visitors enter up the granite steps leading to the three shrines made of brass. The halls were adorned with Russian paintings and paintings of Lord Krishna depicting his life, which lead into the main altar. Devotees could be found manning the library or partaking in the temple rituals. The Vishnu Devi temple was visited most by those on a pilgrimage where people gathered and were everywhere, praying. Vishnu Devi was a divine journey through the Himalayas and legend had it that those who made it through were blessed with the fulfillment of their dreams. It was a place where all barriers were transcended because even the Goddess Mata Vaishno Devi forgave her villain after she beheaded him.

The cave temples were part of his sacred travels, filled with so much beauty that was sadly, unseen and unfathomable

The Great Gathering of Gods Soul

to most of the secular world. He thought of the ancient caves and of modern progression, and it seemed strange that spiritual paths so old could still be more advanced. The old ways still brought peace whereas modern life brought only more suffering. He was blessed to have seen the temples and he worshipped them with gratitude.

He felt such significance in the meaning and symbolism of spirituality, and he was fascinated with the holy places and the manifestation of gods. There were the goddesses Kali, dark and unholy, Lakshmi, sustenance and prosperity, and Saraswati, purity and goodness. Through his learning, he saw the parallels to mankind and these gods. He began to see that wherever a person was in the world, he seemed to have a different way to express the same principals of life. He believed strongly that there must be something to his finding, and it compelled him to search deeper.

The training in love and compassion was endless and it was soothing to his soul. He found peace there at Ashram House; yet he knew there was so much more to be learned from the world outside. He wondered about Christianity, the Muslim faith, Buddhism, Jainism, Shintoism and many other isms he did not yet know even existed. He wondered about philosophy, poetry and even the faith of non-believers, as believing in nothing was also a ritual in the faith of having no faith. He began to need to know what these other ways were about. He could not be content until he understood them all.

One day while he had been waiting to speak with a guru privately about such things, he witnessed the man being held hostage spiritually, so it seemed, by an Evangelical Christian missionary who was debating the teachings of Hinduism verses Christianity. It appeared that the missionary came to save the soul of those in the Hindu faith and the Christian man was noticeably irritated. So, Satya sat silently in the hall awaiting his turn listening.

The Guru sat peacefully and sincerely in the presence of the man and earnestly listened to his questions.

The Great Gathering of Gods Soul

"If you do not believe in Jesus you will go to hell," the evangelical man explained. "You ask for forgiveness of your sins, and they will be forgiven. Do you want to be forgiven?" he asked the guru of the Ashram house.

"Oh yes," the guru replied.

The Christian man looked as if he saw a window of hope for his student's soul and his eyes began to shine with the gleam of salvation.

"Do you accept Jesus into your heart as your Christ and savior," he asked the guru.

"Oh, yes, I do," the guru replied.

Satya watched with intrigue because he did not understand that his teacher seemed to be swayed of his faith so easily into another faith.

The Christian man jumped for joy and began to cheer in celebration. The instructor sat in the same calm and peaceful position watching the religious man yell and scream in elation.

"Do you know what this means?" the missionary asked the guru.

The guru just smiled at him awaiting his answer.

"This means you're saved," the missionary said, calming down and touching the tops of the gurus' hands. The guru sat quietly with his palms down in his lap, watching the Christian man.

"Do you love Jesus?" he asked him to receive a final confirmation.

"Oh yes," the guru said smiling a gentle and calming smile. "And so does Baba."

The man frowned and he became noticeably angry and frustrated, grabbing his things and storming out of the room. Satya laughed quietly under his breath and contemplated what he had heard and seen. It seemed that going to extremes was not the way to a spiritually happy life. Quick joy could turn to frustration in that same twinkling of an eye. He logged the experience in the file of his mind and began to yearn for more information of other philosophies and cultures. He wanted to

67

learn what drove others in their zeal for God and he wondered what they knew.

The guru looked and saw him sitting there and walked over to him.

"So, what was the lesson, young man, in what you have just witnessed?" he asked thoughtfully and with a tranquil ease.

"Well," Satya replied. "Life seems to be a series of struggles between balance and extremes."

The guru put his hands on his chin, showing quiet contemplation.

"I was reminded of a book I read many years ago. In the book, while meditating by a stream, the character of the book heard the voice of a Sitar teacher passing by on a small riverboat. The instructor on the riverboat told his student that if he loosened the strings too much it would not play. If he pulled the strings to tight they would break. He said that the way was the middle way, not in extremes. This was not a lesson in playing the Sitar, as I perceived it, but a lesson in the game of life," he said. "What I saw just now was a man who went to extremes and did not listen but proceeded to try to teach a master. He was in a state of unknowingness."

The guru grinned and nodded with joy as Satya continued, "His easily angered state was evidence of his lack of enlightenment, teacher." Satya spoke with such confidence and reason, and it appeared by the looks of the guru that he was proud of him.

"Yes," he replied. "What you witnessed was the strength of love and compassion. I accepted the other man for his own beliefs, believing that we are all part of love's quilt; one truth perceived many ways. The sacred rule of spirit is this," he said, looking deeply into Satya's eyes "Never invalidate a man's beliefs or make him wrong. All paths lead a man to where his journey must take him to grow and learn, and we cannot control that, nor should we want to," he said. "Some will only ever find one path, and some, will find many. That is not for us to decide. It is only for us to love and understand that we are all a family of humanity," he said. "Try to remember that Satya because it is very important. There are three ways in which man seeks to know God: Through religion, through philosophy, and the last is through good deeds and good works. Yet all three paths, although very different indeed, merge into the same desire to know God and have a higher purpose to life and understanding the reason for life's suffering. Remember this, Satya, and it will keep you from ever becoming judgmental with the enlightenment you obtain."

Satya absorbed his wise words and felt grateful to be in the presence of such greatness.

"You are a special one indeed, Satya and the world will offer you a wealth of knowledge. But it is the unlocking of innate wisdom within, that you are after," he added.

Satya's eyes filled with love for his teacher, and as they began to water he lowered his head in humility, cupping his hands in prayer pressing them to his lips. Satya thanked him for the private lesson and walked back to his room.

Later that night he slept and again came the same dream as it had always been throughout his childhood. He was standing in the white room with the large square, then the elevation began until the square was just a dot in a huge space of nothing-white nothing. But it was the first time in years, since he had become a man, that the dream had occurred. He woke up in the morning and went quickly to Ke'ren and Asha's room where they were engaged in drinking Chai tea and burning fragrant incense.

"Good morning," he said smiling politely, yet urgently. "I must speak with you."

The women's brows creased, and they motioned him over to sit by them at once.

"Yes," Asha asked with concern. "What is it?"

He proceeded to tell them about the dream that he had again and that it was the same dream he had encountered as a child over and over again; a white room with a square in the middle of the room. As always he would feel himself rising higher and higher above the square in the white room until the square was a miniscule black dot. He asked them if they knew

69

what it meant because although the dream was abstract in nature, he felt there must be a message within it.

Ke'ren looked at her mother and said, "Tell him, Mother. It is time."

Satya looked at Asha for the answer. The dream disturbed him; yet he did not know why, not knowing that was disconcerting to him? There was an absolute meaning, but he was not able to decode it.

"Satya, you are too wise for the smallness of this place. There is more for you to learn that we cannot teach you here," Asha said. "You are destined to travel abroad to many schools of thought where you will see more of the world's philosophy than we can teach you here. You will learn a great many things," she said, shaking her head. "This is not your final stop. As for the dream that you have had all your life," she said, "The meaning of it was to tell you that you must look beyond, not just at what is before you, like the square. Distance is power, my son, and a man cannot see all the answers to life when he stands in one place to only see the object before him."

His eyes opened wide as it became so clear. He must shift his perception to see things from a distance to truly understand life's mysteries and others.

"Do you understand what I say to you?" she asked. "This dream has come again because once more, it is time for you to shift your perspective. You must now look out at the world with the knowledge you now know. The world will have changed its color based on your awareness. Your life has been like a snake, shedding its skin for you with each lesson learned, each perception realized to wash away your covering."

Ke'ren stood by and listened to her mother tell him the truth.

"It's time for you to go," Ke'ren said.

Satya sat in the chair and plopped back. "It is true; I know it. I have been feeling restlessness lately."

"Always pay attention to that, Satya," Ke'ren said. "Have faith in the process of life and never stop listening, as you did even as a child. Never forget who you are."

The Great Gathering of Gods Soul

"Who am I?" he whispered to himself.

"You are everything and everything is you," Asha replied.

In the twinkling of an eye, he thought to himself, *oh, how life changes.*

"Have you thought of where you will go next?" Ke'ren asked.

"Yes," he said, staring her in the eyes. "Tibet. I want to learn the Buddhist's way of life."

Asha put her hands together in joy and excitement for his chosen path. "Oh dear, a new journey for you, I am so delighted," she said as she and Ke'ren smiled with glee.

"We will prepare for you to leave tomorrow. You will take one item of clothing on your back, and we will give you water and enough rupees to get you there safely. Remember, the gods are with you, Satya," Asha exclaimed, and then both the women departed from the room. He sat as the tapestry from the window blew outward and he knew it was a sign of his leaving. Once again, as nature had invited him into the home upon his arrival, it was guiding him out just as sweetly and he had faith that more awakening was on the horizon.

Later that evening he had a celebration feast with the women who insisted that they give him a send-off that will fill his belly well, for the many days ahead when he would have the memory of love as he traveled alone in solitude. He thought to himself, *who would know better what he needed than women who have spent their lives in travel and exploration of their souls.*

Packing was simple. He would leave with only the clothes on his back, a small leather bag of rupee that the women insisted on sending him off with, a canteen of water, and a small sack for a book or two to read on the journey. Simplicity was the key.

Their last evening was lovely and filled with reminiscences about how they met and all the memories that they had gained from the time that he had come into their lives.

"We were blessed to have you in our lives, Satya," Ke'ren said and smiled with bitter sweetness. Asha nodded in agreement with a facial expression that showed how she would miss him.

"Well, I suppose I should go now to get some rest before my big day," he said with raised eyebrows. The women agreed. As he looked back at them and smiled, he knew he would never meet two women sweeter than they. They were the kindest women he had ever known.

"I don't want to leave you both," he said, torn with love and affection. "Oh, Satya," Ke'ren said. "You will never leave us, not really" and she touched her heart. "We will never leave you as well, be certain of that."

"You must go now, Satya, it is written," Asha said nodding her head and reassuring him.

Satya agreed, bowing his head in submission and he disappeared into the dark glow of moonlight in his room. He retired for the evening and as time and sleep passed over him, he woke up cold and stared at the ceiling. The moment seemed familiar. His eyes caught the two shadows behind his bed and his mind flashed to that night, that pivotal night of mysticism as a child, when he woke in the same manner and froze in fright, scared of the shadows behind him. Yet, this time he was a man afraid of nothing and was not about to let another experience with the shadows of the night pass him by. But before he fully turned his head around to see what stood in the darkness, the shadows moved around from behind him and came to his side. It was the two women that he held in deep affection--Asha and Ke'ren.

"It was you?" he said softly in his sleepy state.

"Things are not always what they seem," Ke'ren replied quietly.

"But…how…that was so long ago when I was a child. It's not possible that you were there. Yet, I have just seen you come from the shadows with my own eyes. The same image from my childhood and you are quit real. My mother said it was my imagination. I believed her," he thought with regret.

"Is this a dream?" he asked.

The Great Gathering of Gods Soul

"It is all a dream, Satya," Ke'ren said. "Merrily, merrily, merrily, merrily, life is but a dream," she sang softly, mimicking the ancient children's lullaby.

"What is life, Satya, if not a dream?" Ke'ren said. "Believe what thine eyes see, beloved," she said holding his chin dearly in one hand. For you have the gift of truth and truth can set a man in shackles, free."

Then Asha began, "There has not been a time when we have not known you, Dear One," and the two women bowed before him.

Then Ke'ren spoke as she raised her head, reached for his hands, and pulled him close to her. "This will be the last time you will see us, but we will be with you always. " she said with tears in her eyes.

Asha came to him and kneeled down on her knees next to the bed. "Remember the feeling in the tree house, Satya? Sensing us in your room as you looked out the window at the silver sky, in your dreams and with your father? We have always been there, and we will always be here for you," she said smiling so kindly that his body became warm from the inside out and all the muddled recollections of his childhood suddenly made sense.

"Another is coming," Ke'ren said with a childish grin, and there before his eyes they disappeared into the shadowy night.

He sat there on the bed wondering if what had just occurred was a dream, although he knew in his heart that it wasn't. He knew he had to begin to trust himself and his visions. He closed his eyes and reminisced about all his childhood memories that were good, and he was filled with hope and love. He saw the women there in his childhood so clearly. Then, he could not see them, but he felt the presence of them and perhaps now he was awakened enough to manifest what was there all along. He lay back in bed thinking and soon fell back into a trance-like sleep, contemplating his thoughts and feeling as though a part of his past had completed itself.

At dawn he woke up and looked out into the distance and saw the rising of the sun. The house was silent.

He dressed in his white linen pantsuit that flowed like the breeze that had always run through the house. He put on the coin bag filled with rupee and the bag filled with bread, water and the three books that Asha had given him. He walked through all the halls that had been his home for many years stopping at the room that smelled of patchouli, which had been Asha and Ke'ren's room. But the room had changed. It was filled with beds for other students who were still asleep, and he knew at that moment that Ke'ren and Asha were never part of the physical world he lived in but belonged to the endless spirit world. He was able to see a world that others could not see, and it was a gift he had been given. He smiled and walked on knowing that once again he was forced to recognize his ability and blessing of seeing beyond the realities of the world. He thought of the walk to the Hotel Santo and the suite he stayed in. He had just walked into the suite, perhaps it was empty and left unlocked or perhaps it was divine intervention? He thought of the airline ticket he was given to India; it could have been by mistake. The Hotel limousine could have been for all guests that stayed at the Hotel and were going to the airport. He remembered the first-class seat he sat in alone with no one by his side. He remembered the driver that held up the sign that said Ashram House, whom *he* had approached. And all the study he did while he was there, because all the people were welcome to study and learn. When he looked back, all that had occurred he had done on his own accord physically but was guided by divine intervention. The women had been there in spirit all along. He saw what others could not see; he saw his divine guidance and he was stunned with humility and gratitude.

The women came into his life and through their love he was able to surpass the physical world to reach out for something more. He was determined to share what he had learned with the world to help them in any way he could. Although others did not have his gift of sight, it didn't feel right that they could not share in the knowledge and peace it could bring. So, he understood that his journey was to help others with his knowledge of awareness and help those who were blind see again. He would share love with those who had none. He had learned through the women to love beyond the physical and through such a teaching his love became infinite. He believed it was selfish to keep such love to himself.

As he walked out the front entrance, passing the flowing drapes and smelling the scent of the sandalwood incense that was joining the wind, he began to walk the dirt road out on his journey, smiling and taking a deep breath. As he passed the life-sized statue of Baba he noticed something that he had not seen before. Behind the statue, there was a tiny golden plaque under the statue. It read, "In loving memory of Asha and Ke'ren Golpalroa, who donated this home for the love of mankind." He remembered the words Asha once told him saying, "Never look back." He felt no sadness because he was filled with their love and they were with him then as they had been there always, all his life.

Chapter Six

Journey Towards Tibet

The journey towards Tibet was long and day after day he watched the sun rise and fall, smelling the fresh air. He slept under trees, and when in the company of strangers, he was often invited into huts, shacks or houses to partake of the local food and drink. He had no regret at being on the road because his life had become an adventure. He had already been through the worst in his life as he saw it. Nothing was so adverse that it would scare him away. He felt at home on the road, absorbing the beauty of nature and the sounds it made. He listened to the birds chirping in the trees and watched them fly from tree to tree, visiting other birds and gathering food for their loved ones. He was fond of the outdoors, especially the fresh air in the morning, and how the oxygen from the plant life felt good, going into his lungs. The air was pure and clean, and it was nothing like the populated cities. He noticed the small creatures, including the bugs, and they all had a sense of direction, just as he did.

But nothing prepared him for the bottomless feeling of loneliness with only his thoughts and memories to keep him company. He had never experienced complete aloneness and it was difficult for him to bear. He relied on his connection with nature, gliding him from one direction to the next, paying attention to his intuition for guidance on which roads to take. He had learned to follow the internal heat of his body as a sign. He was alone and sometimes solemn but felt the solace of the trees and the birds, as well as the many ground creatures he came in contact with. He spent his time considering teachings that were bestowed upon him through life lessons at the Ashram House. He spoke to the women in his dreams and out loud, although they would not reply.

As he traveled throughout India towards Tibet, his kindness and wise counsel along the way deemed him recognition as a man on a pilgrimage, a sort of holy man. His manner of dress was simple and there was no mistaking him for anything else than a man who journeyed for the soul's meaning. He was fed and sheltered on his journey by those who were faithful worshippers of God and so he was sustained, once again, by the kindness of strangers and he never took it for granted. He remembered Asha's voice in times of solitude saying, "The gods are with you." His soft-spoken gratitude was apparent to all whom helped him, and so he was always sent away with food for the road and his canteen full with water. Money was scarcely needed.

But in between the villages and the conversations with others, somber memories would creep into his heart, and he would feel the spite of his loneliness. He'd think thoughts filled with old painful memories and longings. Days would pass in solitude, and he would become desperate to interact with others to avoid the recollections of his mind. He read, thought of philosophy, of things he wanted to learn and would think of conversations with others. Yet, he found the road's cure to silent insanity was to fill his mind and spirit with the love he felt when he was with Ke'ren and Asha. When he thought of them, he was not bothered. The contentment would last for a short period of time before the anxiety of silence would begin. His subconscious mind continued to bring up the painful memories of his past like a secret villain plotting against him.

Through every town and village, he read his books and soon realized that it was not wise to carry so many books on his journey because they became very heavy to carry over long periods of time. So, he produced a plan that would allow him to read many books yet carry only one at a time even though he had little money.

Each village his path would cross, he began to trade his book for another book he had not yet read. By this means he was able to read many books and became well versed on many diverse subjects. He read poetry, religion, philosophy, fiction,

The Great Gathering of Gods Soul

biographies of spiritual and non-spiritual world leaders, sacred prophecy, dogma, ancient healing methods and the lives of prophets and saints. He counseled many with his subtle wisdom and kindness and did all he could to earn the kindness bestowed upon him by others in the only way he could.

After spending many months on the road traveling to reach his destination, he crossed the Ganges River and found himself walking down a dirt road in a place called Bhutan. Hanging everywhere were prayer flags representing the five elements of earth, wind, fire, air and ether. Red, green, yellow, blue and white flags littered the rooftops, mountains and hills signifying a deep respect and sacredness for nature and the culture of the people. As he walked, dogs and cats filled the dirt roads and were more prevalent than the people, yet the people did not seem to notice. The dogs appeared to belong to everyone and no one in particular, looking and smelling dirty. He had never seen so many domestic animals on the streets before and he used caution when they came near.

He had taken his last sip of water the evening prior and had begun to feel weak from thirst. Then a breeze came that smelled of flowers blowing in from a nearby rhododendron bush and suddenly he was rejuvenated. He thought of Ke'ren. He looked to his right and saw the most beautiful bushel of white flowers he had ever seen. As he struggled to continue to walk, he came upon a procession of monks passing under a shady tree. Each monk carried clay jars in the direction of a cave in the lower regions. The remote village where people were present was in the opposite direction from where the monks were headed. He had not seen anyone for almost a week and so he followed the monks respectfully and at a slight distance, observing their ritual which seemed to be the honoring of their dead. Once they had arrived at the cave, incense was lit, and each monk placed a handful of incense above their head while the smoke billowed over the figurines they had placed in the crevices of the cave. They all began to bow in sequence three times, then placed the incense in a pot next to the cave and left them burning there, as they turned back up the road toward the monastery. He suddenly felt revived with excitement.

Although the monks noticed him beyond any doubt, there were no words spoken to him. He followed them and was welcomed in that way, not as a guest but as one who was already part of their group. As they walked up the road for a good while they came upon the monastery and although he was tired and faint his breath was taken by the beauty and essence of the place. The whiteness of the monastery stood out from the tall, green trees that surrounded it. It was cooler and easier to breathe the closer that they got. He was in awe of its amazing stature. It was not just the beauty of the architecture but also the spirit of the atmosphere surrounding the land it lay upon. There was utter peace hovering over the monastery that they called *Kingdom in the Clouds.*

At the entrance of the monastery was a watchtower and immense prayer wheel. As they began to enter the monastery the monk at the door bowed to him, tapped his arm and pointed his finger to go in a different direction than the monks in procession. His lips were dry and cracked, his brown curls were in dread locks and his clothes were soiled from the dirt of the roads. Instantly aware of his desperation he managed to say, "Water."

The monk saw his parched condition and fetched him a cup of water. As he gave it to him, he made a motion for him to drink a small amount only. Satya obeyed, denying his urge to gulp it down. The monk then took him up the stairs of the monastery, into a room and directed him to a washroom and clothes closet. He was bathed and was given a robe of maroon and gold. He was helped to dress by the monk and after dressing; he clutched his white clothes that were deeply soiled. The clothes were special to him because they held the memory of Asha and Ke'ren.

"I want to keep these and wash them," Satya exclaimed to the monk who seemed to speak no English. The monk understood his attachment to his worldly belongings and nodded with a smile and pointed to a basketful of soiled robes to be washed. Satya felt confident that the monk would return his garments.

Satya bowed in gratitude towards the monk with hands in prayer position. In the monk's native dialect, he motioned with his hands and said a word which seemed to mean, "Come."

So, Satya followed the monk down the stairs to join the others who were all sitting on a hardwood floor waiting to partake of their rice meal. The rice sat in huge wicker baskets waiting to be served. He was brought to a certain monk who was already seated peacefully and who greeted Satya with a kind boyish smile. The young monk on the floor listened to his instructions and when the old monk finished speaking, he walked away and continued on with his duties. Satya was left there with the younger monk who was watching him and smiling. Satya gazed at his surroundings, slightly uncomfortable, but open to the experience. When he returned his glance back to the monk he was sitting next to, the monk spoke English to him.

"You are blessed by Buddha to be here, you know?" he said with a thick accent. "Foreigners are not allowed in the monastery, and yet you somehow blew in like the wind, effortlessly," he said staring into Satya's eyes and smiling. Satya had not known that something remarkable had occurred. He did not know that his presence was unusual or forbidden.

"Where do you come from?" the young monk asked.

Satya looked at him, still surprised that he spoke English, and that he spoke it well.

"I have been in India for many years and was traveling to Tibet."

"Why Tibet?" the monk asked.

"Well, I am searching the meaning of life and want to know more about God. To do that, I must know all philosophies and religions of life. I have been drawn to learn more about Buddhism."

"So, then it would seem that you have made it to your destination, haven't you?" he replied. "There are few foreigners that make it into Bhutan each year, yet somehow you have made it through the gates of our Kingdom," he said, causing Satya to consider its significance. "We are monks. Your path has brought you here. You may learn Buddhism here if you choose. Do you choose?" he asked Satya with a twinkle in his eyes.

Satya looked around and suddenly felt comfortable and had the feeling that where he was now, was the place he had been traveling to all along. His arrival in Bhutan happened quite naturally, and he had learned to follow the path that life leads him too, knowing that he was always lead to a particular place for a reason.

"Yes, I would like to stay for a while if that is all right?"

"Yes," the monk said as they both received their portion of rice, chili and cheese. "You will live as one of us and learn our ways?" he asked Satya.

"Yes," Satya replied. "I wish to learn everything there is to learn here. I will work for my stay; whatever I need to do to help you here while I learn."

The monk smiled and seemed pleased with Satya's character, and they began to eat.

"You must know our native tongue, Satya. It will help you learn, as some of the Dharma cannot translate into English well. If you stay, it will benefit you to know the language and have the ability to speak with all the monks here who can share their wisdom. Not all speak English. I imagine that you will also learn to digest our famous chili and cheese dish that is sure to wreak havoc on your digestive system," the monk said with a laugh to point out its spicy nature. Satya tasted its deliciousness and found its spices and flavor to be superb, and also very hot, as he said.

"Where I have come from in India I learned to speak Urdu and Sanskrit. I can learn quickly," he said to the monk. The monk smiled with assurance, and they finished eating in silence.

It had been a long day for Satya, and he was beginning to feel fatigued. Sleep began to call as was common when he had real shelter before him and a place to feel completely safe. He felt safe at the Ashram and now at the monastery, and it was what he had longed for all his life. It dawned on him in a moment's time that all he had longed for had been granted to him now that he had completely forgotten about it. Through his indifference he was granted his wish. He pondered the thought of how the feeling of comfort came so easily now and with no grand entrance. The kindness of others silently healed a portion of his life that held so much pain all his young life. He understood that it was in the complete lack of relying on anything, worldly or otherwise, that he was able to let go of everything. When he did, he was then gifted all for which he had longed. He contemplated while walking up the stairs with the young monk and back into the bedroom they called a kuti where he had been earlier.

Looking at the statue of the laughing Buddha, the monk said out loud, "Do you *know* why Buddha laughs?" Satya shook his head no.

"Because the truth is so simple it is absurd," the young monk said, smiling and nodding. Satya touched the Buddha statue's face as he passed by it and thought to himself how clever his new monk friend was. Truth seemed to be hidden in simplicity.

In the same kuti he noticed that the basket of robes was gone, as well as his clothing. He focused on letting go of his anxiety about not receiving them back and decided that he would dedicate himself solely to the experience at hand. He realized that to let something go causes it to flow back, and so he did not think of them again. He sat on the bed and lay down to rest his tired eyes and fell asleep with a full belly, quenched thirst, and the night sounds of the insects and animals outside.

Early the next morning the monk who had spoken with him over the noon- day meal woke him up, and Satya instantly realized that he had never asked the monk his name. He didn't know what to call him and from surprise he sat up quickly. At the same time the monk made a hand gesture to Satya to stay calm as he maintained a joyous smile on his face that seemed to show his good nature. He was different then the other monks who showed little to no facial expression. This monk smiled often and mostly around him.

"I'm sorry," Satya said to the young monk. "I don't know your name."

The Great Gathering of Gods Soul

"Yava," the monk replied, bowing his head slightly.

"You must wake for the pindapata. We will enter the city to collect food and alms from the villagers." Satya looked at him confused. "The villagers give to us to honor and support our life, dedicated to Buddha. Pay attention and observe our ways. Then later, when we return, you will learn the rice crops."

"I thought I was going to learn..." Satya started to say and was quickly cut off by Yava.

"Yes, yes, trust, trust," he said tapping Satya's hand. "The lessons are in the rice." Satya held back his laughter and smiled at the little monk and although he was confused, he asked no further questions. He just smiled at the funny monk who spoke in riddles. He felt good around Yava, the monk who had such a cheerful nature.

As Satya got up, the monk pointed to the robe he was to wear and then left the room and waited outside the door. Satya put on the robe and Yava was waiting for him with a bright smile. He and the monks went out of the monastery, where they began their tour through the village. They were greeted with genuine love and affection from the people and were given rice, flowers, spices and many other things the Buddhist's could use in their daily life. Satya watched as some family members of the Buddhist's came up quickly, to hug their brothers or sisters, and it was then, he knew that this way of life would be favorable to him. He observed their ritual and as he did, he felt free, he was happy.

As they returned to the monastery, Yava began speaking. "We harvest rice." He informed him. "Today you will begin your lesson with the birth of seedlings."

Satya was intrigued. He knew he would be receiving an education, worldly and otherwise, but had never imagined that he would learn to cultivate rice.

They walked out of the monastery and into the fields. Everywhere his eyes could see there was beauty, the greenery, pink and white flowers, colored prayer flags and the sound of birds singing. The monks and government officials who shared the monastery worked together to cultivate and harvest the rice,

The Great Gathering of Gods Soul

while staying apart of any of their practices. Satya and Yava surveyed the land while Yava showed him the many workers and what they were doing. He explained that there were two phases of growing the rice plant; the first was the *vegetation* phase and then the *reproductive* phase. He dipped his hand into the huge barrel of rice grain that they were passing as he explained to Satya that all rice started as a seedling.

"There are many stages in the life of the rice plant. As you can see, they start out encased in the hull; much like an embryo is protected in the womb of the mother."

Satya stared at him and listened intently to what he was saying. "Seedlings will lay dormant until they receive the water that brings them to life, and they begin to be nourished. Just like the wisdom from our lives within our cellular structure lies dormant until we are nourished with life-giving water, bringing the realization of who we are and have been," Yava concluded.

"Who are we?" Satya blurted out anxiously as if life gave the answers that easy.

"Oh," Yava laughed. "You must be patient," he said as he began to walk again. Then suddenly, he turned his head back to look at Satya directly behind him and said, "Ancient Bhutanese secret," and they began to laugh incessantly. As they continued walking Satya noticed the labor of the men working and the smell of the sweat and effort that went into the cultivation of the rice.

Then Yava continued, "Under the conditions of the soil, roots begin to develop in the dark. The soil in Bhutan is eroding and it makes it very difficult to grow crops, Satya. Constant care has to be taken for the survival of the rice plants." Satya realized the importance of what Yava was saying because he became very serious and looked worried.

"People are very much like rice crops, Satya. Even in the harshest conditions they will sink their roots deep, develop and grow because change is the only thing that is consistent in this world. Even when their atmosphere is dark, they will still break free from the darkness and sprout forth above the harsh conditions, like rice. Some could say that the darkness is a

84

necessary part of the awakening process. Without a harsh condition, a person, like the seedling, would perhaps never split from the root to reach for a higher ground," he said.

Yava spoke in this manner to him all the daylong and Satya could not help but feel that Yava was speaking to his soul about what he had been through in his life and his will to overcome it all. Yava was a messenger of hope, bringing him understanding of his life's mysteries.

"Here you will learn many things that will carry you farther on your journey if you should choose to go some day. There is something in you I see that is growing and I would be honored to guide you, as long as I am needed," he said respectfully.

"Thank you, Yava," Satya said. "You have spoken to my heart today on many levels."

Yava smiled and replied to him, "From this day forward your learning will be profound. You will begin your instruction in our native language called Dzongkha, and we will start you in the sacred teachings of Buddha, daily, as a novice monk. We will continue to watch the crops while we study. The teachings are in the rice," he said again and smiled.

Satya could do nothing other than smile at the silly yet profound Buddhist monk.

The day with Yava had passed so quickly. He was enthralled with the conversation of the wise young monk and during the day's instruction the sun had risen and crossed over the sky.

"We will go back now to contemplating the life of rice," he said. Then Satya heard the temple bells begin to chime. As they were returned to the monastery Yava said, "It is time for our evening devotions." That evening Satya perceived that a man does not have to believe in God or a single mover of the universe to pray. He learned that prayer was a form of meditation in all cultures and that praying was an innate need to show gratitude and love for life and being part of it.

Many days passed, and as Satya began to feel more at home in his new life as a novice monk he began to see how he stood out from the rest. He did not want to stand out, but wanted to live as they lived without causing them distraction. He wanted to experience the Buddhist life and live it fully, to understand their culture and how they live. He looked at himself in the mirror in his kuti and saw that his hair had grown long and quite curly, to a length past his shoulders. His life as a traveler left little time or need for vanity. Long hair was not conducive to the way of a pilgrim. He had no particular preference to have it long or short, but he now felt a need to cut it so that he would not disturb the monks and remind them of the outside world, that they were not part of. He himself wished to learn and not be distracted, nor be a distraction to others and so he called for Yava. Together they shaved off all his hair. As it hit the floor Yava smiled at him and laughed.

"Bye-bye," he said talking to Satya's hair.

Slightly nervous, Satya mustered only a grin. Yava picked up some of the hair on the floor and showed it to him. "Weaved together," he said referring to Satya's hair, "we can make a sweater for a small child," and he laughed and smiled his ear-to-ear smile. Satya looked at all the hair on the ground and felt an interesting feeling. He thought that perhaps he would have a feeling of remorse or some attachment to the hair but all he felt was a desire to learn and get on with things. He smiled to himself and knew that he would not glance into the mirror again during his stay at the monastery. He wanted to focus more on what was inside now that he was dedicated to learning. He wanted to learn all that he could before his life journey took him somewhere else as it always seemed to do. Satya dressed as Yava spoke of the meaning of each fold in his robe. Then Satya bowed before Yava and Yava took a pinch of uncooked rice and flower petals that sat in his room in a bowl and sprinkled it over Satya's head, initiating his new beginning.

Each day the monks would instruct him and soon he began to learn their language while studying the four hundred and twenty-three verses of the Dhammapada spoken by Buddha.

He was not fluent in their language, but he began using their dialect to respond to the questions. The monks were astonished at how quickly he was learning. Only Yava could speak to him when he first arrived and now he was speaking with almost everyone. Satya was aware of his limitations but his will to learn was strong and so the monks cheered him on softly, with smiles and praise.

He realized that although the Buddhist were mysterious people from the eyes of the world, they were not so different than others. They also required love and attention, a sense of family and encouragement. He found them to be the most accepting people he had ever known and developed a brotherly love for them. The monks looked within themselves to better the world and he liked their philosophy of personal responsibility to do no harm to themselves or to others. What he learned from them was priceless and spiritually altering.

Chapter Seven

From Seedlings to Tillers

After sometime the rituals of the daily life of a Buddhist monk settled in. Like every other morning, Yava came in and woke him in his kuti to rise for the early morning walk for food and alms, or so he thought.

"Wake, Satya, we will go back to the rice fields," Yava said.

Satya woke and began to put on his robe as Yava spoke to him of their plans for the day.

"The seedlings have become tillers," Yava said.

"More lessons in the rice?" Satya said with a smile, rubbing his tired eyes.

"Oh, you're so clever," Yava replied with his thick accent.

Satya had such a fondness for Yava, and he began to see Yava as a brother. Yava was special because he was like a very wise brother whom he could tell all his personal thoughts to and ask questions with ease. Yava always answered his questions as best he could.

They walked through the fields and for as far as the eye could see were the sprouts of tillers that had once been mere seedlings. The plants were growing under conditions of eroding soil, and out of the darkness, surfaced to be seen. As they walked through the dirt and plants, they looked on in joy and amazement, trying to acknowledge the life of all the plants, as if they were people. The plants were like small babies to him that had just been born. He felt such joy in seeing them and knowing that these seedlings that they had helped nourish, would in turn nourish the masses.

For a long period of time they walked, smelling the enriched soil and walked farther than they had walked before. In the near distance he saw a small bridge and shady area with one lone tree filled with glorious red apples and before it was a small man-made pond. Satya said nothing to him and knew that it was surely the place that they were headed. When they reached the tiny wooden bridge they sat on a bench that was open to the water in the middle of it. Yava had two long and thin pieces of bamboo that he pulled out of the satchel he had been carrying on his back. He asked Satya to pull down two long ropey vines from the apple tree that hung over the pond.

As he pulled them off the tree, Yava handed him the thin bamboo that had a crack at the tip and showed him how to slip the ropey stem in between the crack of the bamboo, making what he assumed was a fishing pole.

Satya leaned over and looked into the quaint little pond.

"Are there even fish in there?" he asked.

Yava did not reply, but he finished making his pole. Satya scratched his head in wonder and waited patiently while reaching out to touch the cool water. Even if there weren't any fish, he thought it was fun to pretend there were, and so he went along with Yava.

"Now, cast the rope into the water," Yava said as he threw his rope attached to the bamboo into the pond.

"I don't see any fish in there," Satya said playfully, yet concerned. But Yava said nothing; he only had the smile of sweet bliss on his face and held the pole in fishermen's position. Satya followed the lead of his friend and fished in the same manner.

Then Yava continued on with his training, "Each stem of rice is made up of nodes and internodes," he said, holding his pole steady. "They will vary in length depending on the variety and the environmental conditions. Each node bears a leaf and a bud, which can grow into a tiller. The leaf blade is attached at the node by a leaf sheath. Where they meet is a pair of claw-like appendages called the auricle, which encircle the stem. Coarse hairs cover the surface of the auricle." Yava looked at Satya for a moment.

"That's interesting," Satya said, rather confused.

Yava just smiled at him, knowing that he was capable of a better answer. As Satya began to ask a question, Yava continued, "People, like rice, come in many varieties. They are also surrounded by various environmental conditions and regardless of that, they will bear a leaf and bud of their own. That would be their character. The life of a bud can do many things, as those who have life have many ways they can follow a path of growth. The rice sheath can grow tall and through the roughness of life and circumstance. It will build a claw-like, coarse area around the chamber of their auricle which, to the rice, would be the chamber of their heart."

Satya looked at Yava who was speaking to his heart. Satya had told him the story of his life, and so Yava's instruction was tailored in many ways to his own life, yet true for all life beings, rice and human.

"There is coarseness over the auricle, the heart because it is fragile, as life is fragile. The tillering or growth stage begins in rice and in humans as soon as the seedling or human is self-supporting. That is why your growth began as soon as you made the choice to grow above the dark depths you have known in your childhood," Yava said sincerely, looking intently into Satya's eyes.

Satya's eyes watered and became teary. There had always been a part of him that felt a blade to his heart, anointed with vinegar, for the pain and hurt he had known as a child. Even though he was aware that he would not be where he was now had he not known the blade's sharpness.

"Satya, we all come from a watery deep. We must not forget the darkness but learn to shine even while in it and to keep struggling to break free and rise to the surface, just as the rice does." Yava smiled, waiting for this profundity to sink in.

"Spiritual gems can either hide in darkness, or become voyagers above ground, both liberated by the journey of the soul."

As Yava said those words he began to fiddle with the fishing pole he had made and looked over into the pond. They had been sitting for many hours talking and it was no surprise to Satya that they hadn't gotten even one nibble by a fish.

"I don't think there are even any fish in there, Yava. Besides, you can't catch a fish with nothing on the end of the

The Great Gathering of Gods Soul

pole," Satya concluded. "Why fish in a pond that is empty? What's the point?" he asked.

Yava grinned a grand smile, the largest Satya had ever seen on Yava's face.

"Precisely," Yava said happily. "It's as pointless as fishing for worldly pursuits that do not nourish the spirit. In the end, worldly things give you nothing of importance, they do not nourish the soul, nor do they follow you in death." Then Yava stood up from his seated position and began to pull the rope from the water and packed his and Satya's pole into his bag. They walked back to the monastery and during that time Satya continued to look at Yava with amazement for how wise his Bhutanese brother was. He had never felt so relaxed, happy and focused on the moment. He learned on many levels that day at the pond.

Many months later, Satya had become very accustomed to living in the monastery. He enjoyed the trips into the city, the schooling, the chanting and people- watching during the brief daily visits that his monk brothers had with their families. He watched Yava meet with his parents and brothers and noticed how his mother would bring him one box of cigars per week. On their trips into the city for food and alms every morning Yava would smoke a cigar. Each time, Satya laughed at the look of it; a Bhutanese monk in his robe smoking a cigar. It was almost as funny as watching the few monks who had them talk on their cell phones. It had been almost a century since the first king allowed cell phones into Bhutan.

He helped in the rice fields as well as performing his monastic duties but preferred to be outside the monastery. He enjoyed working in the sun with his hands in the fields, finding it therapeutic and centering. There was something so spiritual to him in watching the birth and growth of something he had helped nurture. While in the fields, he spent much of his time reminiscing experiences in India with Asha and Ke'ren. In his mind he would speak to them, and they would give him guidance and love, silently. He never felt alone. It was as if they were with him the way it had always been, an astral connection.

His relationship with Asha and Ke'ren was no different than the way it was with his father. He no longer doubted if it was imaginary or true. He knew it was real. He understood that those on the other side still loved and wished to communicate with those from whom they had departed. They still had love for those who remained on earth and watched over him.

Many nights as he looked outside before he'd go to sleep, he would think of his mother and send his loving compassion into the night air, hoping it would reach her. He had learned to feel pity and compassion for her sad condition and began to love her, but this time, as a man, with forgiveness in his heart.

He learned the language of the Bhutanese and became fluent. He learned the *Three Jewels of Life,* the *Five Poisons*, the *Six Realms*, the *Three Buddha Bodies* and the *Four Noble Truths*. He was taught the fine art of meditation and how to block out the thoughts in his head that would destroy the sanctuary in his soul. Still, during all this, he would walk daily in the fields to check on his children seedlings that had developed spikelets. When he stepped out onto the field to see them, the whole field had become colorful with violet flowers. The land had gone from a barren, weed-like, colorless place to a sight that would make a godless man believe in something greater than himself. He laughed a joyful laugh that took his breath. His silent tears of joy filled his heart, proud that he had something to do with such goodness. He thought about how people would sit at a table someday to take in the nourishment of the rice and not think of the love that had gone into its development. But there were many on the grounds of the monastery who would know, and he knew that he himself would never again take food for granted the way he had all his life. Especially knowing that even in such harsh conditions and with the constant threat of corroding soil, life sprouted and defied the odds. The way people often did.

During a lesson, Satya became distracted and wanted to know more about his Bhutanese brother.

"Yava, where are you from?"

Yava closed the book they had been looking at for instruction and gave Satya his full attention. It was as though no one had asked him that question before.

"I am Egyptian and Bhutanese. I was born here but my mother is from Egypt." The chair Yava was in made a crackling noise as he shifted into a comfortable position to talk with Satya.

"Why do you ask, my brother?" Yava inquired.

"I want to know you. You aren't like the other Buddhists here."

"Oh, thank you," Yava said, laughing.

"I mean, I have never known anyone like you, and I feel like you are what a brother would feel like, although I have never had any siblings. If I did, I would want him to be you," Satya said sincerely.

"We are all brothers, Satya. But I am very fond of you as well and I understand what you mean. We share a special bond, you and me. We are different in our own way that only we can understand."

Satya nodded his head in agreement and looked down.

"We are absolutes," Yava said.

When Satya heard him say the word *absolute*, it sounded familiar, and he remembered that he had heard his father say something similar to him as a boy.

"My mother used to love words," Yava said smiling to himself while he reminisced. "She would say that absolutes make good monks and if an absolute were to have any relationships, it was rare. It was rare because they looked for is their doppelganger, which is hard to find."

"What is a doppelganger?" Satya asked.

"It is the one person in the world who is just like you, your double. We are unconditioned from the world, Satya, you and me. No matter how much an absolute is in the world, he cannot be domesticated to it and therefore is unconditioned. He is the truth, not the world's version of what truth is. Perhaps this is why you have always felt as though you did not fit in," he said. "It is because you never really did, Satya. Your purpose is grander than that. Absolutes are chosen for a specific reason.

The Great Gathering of Gods Soul

You are on a journey to find out what that reason is, and I am honored to be part of your journey, brother," he said and bowed his head before him.

"We are not our body, Yava. This I know, because I have left it many times and have felt the freeness of one who has lifted the weight of the universe from his back. I have felt before the serenity of no cares, bad memories or thoughts."

"Yes, Satya. This is Nirvana that we wish to attain, the end of suffering. You grow closer to it all the time, with the awareness of who you are. You are limitless, but the mind must be tamed because it controls the body."

Satya nodded his head and looked out the window with the peaceful look he would get when he was leaving his body in a fully conscious state.

"My mother said that the body was the root of all things lost." Yava said. "There was a time when people were aware of their powers to move things with their will, the way they did with the pyramids, but it was lost. Their language was much like the Aryans of Central Asia who spoke a language that contained conceptual images and concepts. They developed inner telepathic and telekinetic insights with their communication. They called them Siddhis-psychic powers.

When her people began to pack physical things in tombs to take to the other side with them, believing that the physical body itself was immortal, then they lost their powers and the awareness of who they really were. The body is not immortal, it is only a vessel carrying the spirit and once passed on to the other side, there is no use for a body or physical things. A spirit is Nirvana or Heaven; it is all, has all, naturally. If only the world could see that."

Then Yava said, "The body confines the spirit, but when controlled and understood, the spirit can leave willfully because the body has no immortal power. The spirit of man is the power. It is much the same belief in Buddhism. You are not a body but so much more, you are the universe. While always remembering, to do no harm to ourselves or to others and understand that teaching, so that you may reach the awareness that nothing is learned or unlearned, awareness just is. There is no need for lessons when you know what you know," Yava said as a matter of fact.

Satya looked at Yava with revelation and felt so pleased to know him since he had become such a great friend and teacher. At times he felt a surge of surrealism, grateful for what he had learned and for where he had been. Going all the way back to his childhood, he knew that each experience led him to the other and it all was necessary. He knew that if one single element of his life were changed, it would alter everything. So, he learned to be grateful for all his experiences, especially those that were the most painful.

He had learned a very important lesson in life. He learned that when he sought out his destiny, the universe seemed to conspire to help him find it. The Universe seemed to foreshadow events that were to come. He decided then and there that he would be on the watch at all times for what the universe, that is, all that is in creation, was saying to him through signs and visions.

Daily, they continued to walk the fields to help nurture the land, but the soil was becoming difficult to cultivate. The rice plants were in their vegetative state and the condition of the soil was crucial for their development. For days, there had been trouble with the sprinkler systems not working correctly, and the monks and field technicians worked harder than ever to manually bring the water to the areas of the crops where the water was not reaching. Satya found himself caring for the plants as if they were his own children and bringing them much needed food for their survival. They filled large jugs full of water and designated areas for the monks to form an assembly line to get the water manually to where it needed to go. It was a backbreaking, horrific feat to undertake but he did it for the survival of the rice plants.

Weeks of this type of watering continued while the monks and workers tried to fix the sprinkler system. Then the inevitable occurred. The sprinkler system shut down all together. The rice plants were dying, and Satya knew it. The monks did what they could to save the crops, but they could not fight it any longer. They were exhausted, and although their means of life relied on the rice crops, they accepted the failure as a sign of karmic debt and seemed saddened but content to accept their fate. Heartbroken by the slow death of his seedlings, Satya went into his kuti emotionally drained, skipping the evening devotions. He went to sleep with a heart heavy with helplessness.

Then, as soon as he fell asleep, he woke to a dream state, still in his room. He was in his bed and Asha, Ke'ren and his father were standing there at his feet. He sat up, happy to see them but he felt a sense of urgency from them. They seemed to have little time for pleasantries. "Father," he said with happiness.

His father looked at him with warmth in his eyes and said to him, "Look to the sky, Satya," and he pointed out the window, showing the rising of the sun.

Satya creased his brow, not understanding what his father was telling him. Then Ke'ren lowered to her knees at the foot of his bed saying, "Go now to the fields, HE is waiting." She was looking out the window intently, looking at the sun coming up. Then quickly, the room turned white, and he saw the square and began floating. He did not understand what Asha, Ke'ren and his father were trying to say to him. Suddenly he was jolted from his sleep with a feeling that something was going to happen in the fields. Desperate and panicked over what he did not know, he jumped to his feet, threw on his robe and began to make a rustling noise as he ran through the monastery waking up the monks with the sound of crackling wood from his running feet on the floor. Because that sound was scarcely heard in the monastery, Yava came out of his kuti, seeing Satya's behavior. In minutes, many of the monks were following closely behind him as he ran out the front door and into the fields.

When he reached the field he looked at the vastness, and for as far as his eyes could see, the rice plants were hanging over. They were no longer able to support themselves from the lack of water and decaying soil. He knew the death cycle had set in and

The Great Gathering of Gods Soul

it was now too late to save them. His emotions were filled with sorrow, injustice, hopelessness, helplessness, and in the end, rage. He felt rage for the seedlings and for everything in his life that had ever gone wrong. He allowed himself to feel the powerful release of his anger. As his eyes filled to the brink of overflow, he looked at the orange and yellow sun coming up in the pink sky, and with an outcry like never before, he screamed to the Heavens with his arms raised as though pleading, "WHY?" He screamed as he fell to his knees, holding his face in his hands and sobbing like a child. It was a cry from the belly of his soul.

The monks watched him, touched with compassion but they did not know how to help his pain. Yava walked toward him and touched his shoulder to console him when a drop of rain hit his nose. Yava stopped and put his palm up toward the sky and Satya's cry froze in disbelief. Satya had seen the drop of water hit his face. Then at once, the sky opened up to his cry and rain like they had never seen before in Bhutan poured down. Satya rose to his feet and began to laugh in gratitude and thanksgiving. The universe had listened to his cry for help. He looked at all the monks and they laughed joyfully as they put their hands out to feel the rain in their hands, and they all became soaked with the redeeming rain, lost in their laughter. Satya knew then and there that the crops would survive.

For many days after the incident there was a feeling of uncharacteristic joy and mysticism in the monastery. As they all continued on with their daily rituals they understood that something powerful had happened in the fields that they could not explain, nor did they try. They showed their gratitude by continuing to nurture the crops.

One night after dinner Yava and Satya walked in the evening sun to check the crops that had been saved and to take a peaceful stroll. Satya felt the happiness of life's seasons in the fields. He realized that whether blood or grain, the process of life was the same for all. Birth, suffering, awakening and finally, death were all the same. He came to find that the Four Noble

Truths of suffering were correct. That the less he craved the less he suffered. He believed that suffering could end if he followed a path of right view, right thought, right speech, right action, right livelihood, right effort, right mindfulness and right concentration. Death in itself, was life begun anew, whether in Nirvana or in the world. He believed that non-suffering *could be* attained.

"As you have seen, Satya, the vegetative phase is very important and is when most of the growth occurs. The blossoming of the flower signifies growth and then, and only then, does it reproduce. Many things can interfere with development and also with reproduction," Yava said as he walked. Satya listened silently while walking next to him.

"These plants are just like people, Satya. The environment they are surrounded by can indeed offer a challenge to their growth. But when they fight for their survival, they can reproduce and bare beautiful fruits, blossoming flowers and nurture a nation." Then he stopped walking and faced Satya. "You are a testimony to that, Satya. You have been just like the rice plants we have watched grow, suffer, die and be reborn. You have entered through many stages, endured the harsh environment and have refused to give up without a fight, for the sake of goodness. What you did for the rice is what you have been doing your whole life--fighting for survival."

As Yava spoke those words, Satya felt the ball in his throat tighten, feeling such love and gratitude for the kindness that Yava had always bestowed upon him and the acknowledgement Yava had for what he had been through. He felt thanksgiving and mere hugs or kisses would not be enough to repay him for all he had given.

"There is always a choice, Satya. You made a choice in your own life to fight, and in character, you fought for the seedlings to live as well. Because you fight for good, the universe rewards your efforts. You have a gift to fight the wrongs of the world and win. You must share your gifts of wisdom as an inspiration for others, so they continue on their path of endurance." Satya listened to his friend's words and knew their

The Great Gathering of Gods Soul

efficacy would change his life forever. They continued on walking until sundown and then retired to their routine of the evening.

Satya stayed on in the monastery for many years after that and lived the Buddhist life, inundating himself with truths of the soul. He began to see that life was a series of constant change and that change was the only thing he could count on. He learned that although all walks of life were so different, all had three things in common. He believed that all mankind sought a teacher to learn from, a teacher to live by, and a community to belong too. He understood more about the world through the teachings of those three jewels of life. He understood that in desperateness to belong or fit in somewhere, people would even choose a world that was dangerous and criminal. Mankind had a need for belonging that was so deeply rooted that it had to be innate to want to be loved by a family.

He felt at ease with his thoughts and over time with the monks he continued to learn and apply all the teachings to the condition of life. He learned that life was a path of distractions, and that people were drawn to the power of chaos. He believed that the challenge of life was to retain the energy chaos posed, while keeping it in its place. He deduced that there was no perfection in life, or in people, but the closest thing to it was awareness. Perfection to him was awareness wrapped in goodness and spirituality. He thought about how people were lost or hiding in the darkness of themselves because they refused to wake up from their long sleepwalk through life. He thought how their lives could be radically changed by the single thought. The idea that they had the ability to create the universe they decided and could realize who they really were. He learned that all absolute theories of the soul were a hindrance of a good life because people became stuck in their identity of whom and what they *think* they are. The world had become unaware and unwilling to accept the only thing in life that was constant change.

99

His world was enhanced and changed by his stay at the monastery, and he began to believe that there was so much more that he could do in the world to help others than to live in the monastery in solitude. He felt he had truths that he could share with others who might listen and be touched by them, or perhaps even have a better life. He believed that the truths he learned there were not singular to being Buddhist, but more to being human. Because no matter what the teaching was called or where it came from, the meaning was the same. The stories and the myths were all the same. All mankind suffers life and death, all people wish for meaning to their lives and all mankind struggles to understand the world and how to survive it. It did not matter what culture a person was raised in, to him all mankind suffered the same. His eyes became clearer than they had ever been before, and all the things that he had minimal understanding of now seemed to awaken in him. Yet, it did not feel like a new truth, but one that was awoken from its long, dead sleep. He knew that his life could have so much more meaning if he followed what was in his heart to do; to journey elsewhere to awaken people everywhere, one person at a time.

Although he felt so much peace at the monastery, he began to feel that his life's purpose was no longer being fulfilled there. It did not seem right to hold such gifts inside him when they could benefit so many. He believed that if he could help even one person than he must make the journey to find that one. He hoped to better the life of others and believed that even one man was worth a journey of a thousand miles. There was to much to learn, so many ways to live and so much desire to help that he could no longer deny it.

One day while preparing the rice in the cookers, Satya spoke to Yava.

"Yava," he said with hesitation while looking down at the rice cooker. "I must leave you now."

Yava looked at him with a knowing glance, nodding as if he already knew.

The Great Gathering of Gods Soul

"Yes, I knew this day would come," he said as he put down the stirring stick and faced him. "There are two kinds of people, Satya, Saints and Worldlings. You are a Bodhisattva, Satya. You have delayed your right to Nirvana to help the world that needs you. You will guide many to their path. I had always known that you would go. I wish you wouldn't go because I know that you will never return. But it is your destiny and so you must. There are so many others that will see your guiding light and get back onto a path of righteousness and hope. You must go at once." Satya was not surprised by his brother's words. Yava was what he imagined a true brother to be.

"We will prepare you for the journey in the morning," Yava said with glistening eyes. They hugged and then returned to their task at hand, neither saying another word for the rest of the evening.

That morning at dawn's early light he woke to see Yava standing over him. As he did, he rose up. Yava held out his white linen suit that he had not seen in many years and had even forgotten about. In the other hand he held his water canteen that had been filled, his sack filled with bread and cooked rice, and his coin purse, slightly fuller than when he arrived.

As he dressed there was quietness in the room from all the emotions he was feeling but did not say. Words were not needed. As they walked, his monk brother put his arm around him. When they got to the front monastery door, to his surprise, all the monks were assembled facing the sunrise that was coming up over the mountain. They had left a path for him to walk down the center, and as he and Yava walked to the front gates down the dirt path, Satya looked at all the men, women and young ones who were dressed in their burgundy and gold robes and held small prayer wheels in their cupped hands. He smiled at them trying to see them all for one last time. They smiled back at him as he made his way through, and when he reached the gate they all raised their prayer wheels above their heads and began to bow to him turning their wheels signifying the turning of doctrine in his life.

Satya was touched and felt many emotions of love for all his brothers and sisters in the monastery, knowing that he would never see them again in his lifetime. Yava hugged his brother for the last time and then stepped back with the other monks. Satya watched him light his incense that he had in his robe and bowed three times before him to honor and bless his journey. Touched by the moment and torn by human attachment to stay, he smiled at them all and with a twinkle of his eye to Yava he turned and began to face the long dirt road he came on. Only this time it was to take it in another direction for a new life experience.

He knew that he would learn a great many things, meet a great many people and witness many glorious and tragic things along the way. What he understood was that the most important thing was that his life had a purpose, and that purpose was to seek enlightenment for the sake of others. He could not be content unless he was sharing what he had learned. So, he listened to the voice of the universe and humbly traveled on his journey paying attention to the signs, listening to the small voice inside and healing all those he could along the way.

There were many meanings to his life as a monk and a Hindu. Traveling in solitude had become much easier than it had been before, and it was because he had learned to quiet the belittling voice of his mind that used to taunt him so. He had acquired an inner peace and no longer questioned his life's purpose. He had seen the wisdom in the experiences of his life and realized that they made him who he was, all of which he could not have become had his suffering not occurred. He realized that suffering was inevitable and would continue, although awareness of suffering's purpose made it less treacherous.

He believed that each life had a divine purpose that sadly was often unrecognized. As time passed, he learned a great many things and traveled to a great many places. Always, one journey lead to the next. He passed through so many places that he could no longer number them. Through each region he saw suffering and troubles, culturally, economically and religiously.

The Great Gathering of Gods Soul

He survived rains of sand in the desserts, famine, drought, hurricane and flood. He experienced hospitality and joy, but also persecution and abusive treatment for his life as a traveler. Belonging to no sect, race or religion he was both accepted and ostracized from place to place. Through all his joys and suffering he continued to feel invigorated for having made the choice to grasp life with both hands and be in the game of life.

Through each path he crossed, came the repeated childhood dream signaling him that it was time to move on to another place to help others who were in need. Each time the dream occurred; he traveled on leaving one city in search of the next. He studied the people in each region with their religions and philosophies along the way. Each religion and philosophy added to his belief that all mankind were the same. Each story, history and philosophy increased his love for mankind and inspired him to continue on selflessly, to help others realize who they were and of what they were capable. He endowed himself a slave to mankind's purpose hoping to lead the thirsty back to the water well. He would revive the teaching of compassion that had been lost so long ago. He wanted to lead mankind by the example of love, removing all boundaries or divisions between them.

He no longer suffered the chaos of his own mind, and so he traveled endlessly in peace more effectively than ever to listen and help heal the masses. He traveled to faraway places, in search of any person whose energy called out to him for help. And help he did for everything he touched was meant to be.

Chapter Eight

The Condition of the World

Satya, more mature but still a young and simple man followed a ritual path, always leading from one city to the next helping those in need. His style was non-threatening, and kind and he gave the type of counsel that caused an individual to look within himself to find the answers to life. His advice was the kind that caused people to accept accountability for their own happiness. He sat in on many family counsels, heard family members blaming others for their actions. He was firm and truthful with his advice and because of that was respected. He would explain that no person was in control of another person's reaction. It was a person's choice to give away his control and give in to the passion of anger. Always he would finish with the instruction, "Physician, heal yourself." His words were down like a hammer and landed with a velvet touch. His words were smooth but firm and heavy and demanded self-reflection.

Having no connection to his mother any longer, and all his family of choice were in the spirit world, his roots were not firmly planted anywhere in particular. The lack of blood ties was a shortcoming that he realized was actually a blessing to his sacred task in life. He was to seek out those who needed knowledge and enlightenment so they might live a peaceful life. For that purpose, he had to be free of all attachment. Peace was something that came in abundance to him since he had cleared all his own demons. So, he eagerly and willfully shared his outlook on life with others and the wisdom of experience that got him there.

He found himself exposed to philosophies of life that he had never known before, and it excited him. He traveled from Bhutan to China, China to Mongolia, Mongolia to Russia and into Europe. From the spice markets of India, the rice crops of Bhutan, through the long saltwater rivers and icy winters of

Northern Asia, to the southern year-round warmth and heavy summer rains, to the extreme wealth and poverty of Russia, he continued to learn.

He learned that each ethnic group had its own languages, customs and appearance. He saw how Asia alone had so many languages that even neighbors had a difficult time understanding one another. He began to see why so many people divide and judge one another, especially in their religious and philosophical beliefs. They failed to seek the most important thing in life to attain greater good; communication. He learned that some cultures were very prone to social opinion, schooling, materialism and the appearance of things, while others were consumed with food and drink or immersed themselves in cultural dance and joyful customs. He kept company for a short time, with a man who taught him the sacred, treasure text healing techniques of Reiki and added the knowledge to his storage of goodness. Although in many places he found himself the teacher, there were many times were he became the student, sometimes concurrently. He saw firsthand the anger of cultures and the people within them who would not accept others because they feared what they did not understand. Through all his travels, far and wide, he absorbed each culture and soon he became a seasoned man and traveler. Each time he became less fulfilled with his ability to change their judgmental and combative nature.

He was a pilgrim on a sacred pilgrimage that deepened his faith with each effort he made to help mankind. But with each gift of wisdom he imparted, the more he felt he was not doing enough. It became a process he could understand; it was his foundation, security and his entire reason for being. He was not a psychic as some had called him, but a seer who learned to read the language of the world and had the gift of translating that language into love for others. He taught others how to love themselves so that they might go on to love the world as he did. To those whose lives he had touched, he was a saint.

Now, at age thirty-three, he had nothing but kindness to show for his life's work. His skin was as golden brown as one who labored all day in the sun. His eyes were as blue as the ocean and large enough to reveal the wisdom within his soul. He was tall and masculine, and despite his handsome, godlike appearance, he was as humble as one who had never placed any importance on the exterior of man.

His white flowing linen suit blew in the hot breeze as he looked up to the sky in wonderment. The sun was setting in his favorite orange-and-yellow sky and, like so many other times before, he wondered why, with such beauty that the world was capable of, had God allowed suffering to go on for so long?

As he began to approach the city he was always amazed at how the slight feeling of tingling ran through his body. Amazed at how he could hear from the distance the slight sound of buzzing from the town ahead. He could almost smell the culture by the spices of each area and could get a sense of what their moral diet was by the way each town made him feel. Some warm, some cold, always, his intuition proved to be correct. Walking into the village he could smell the flowers bursting with their sweet aroma and watched the playful birds drinking their nectar. He could sense a general happiness of the people but was never fooled by the appearance of things. In each town he knew there was someone who was in deep pain and disillusionment. When he reached a new village it had a purpose and for that he always continued on his journey.

As he entered the beautiful town of Siena, was blessed with the view of the rich landscapes and he felt happy to see and smell the life of their land. He thought of the vineyards he had passed along the way that created the sweet wine, no doubt, used for their celebrations of love and festivals. And he thought happy thoughts of the town and the dirt road that turned into cobblestone and led him into the city. He was greeted by a powerful and gothic cathedral made of white and black marble. Never before had he seen something so medieval, yet he had seen a great many things equally beautiful and mysterious looking. Cathedrals always sent a chill through him because he would have a quick remembrance of the one he had been left in.

The Great Gathering of Gods Soul

As he continued down the road, he heard the angelic sound of one classical guitar, and then another. One played the lead while the other embraced it in unison with its rhythm. The melody pulled him into the small café where the musicians played and so he stopped there for refreshment and to rest his tired feet. He had been walking the dirt road for some time and was happy to have made it to the next village before the sun had set. He wiped the sweat from his brow as he approached the cashier and flashed a smile that could light up a room, asking her, "May I have a glass of water and a bowl of your Minestra di riso e fave, please?"

The cashier did not seem to mind that he asked her to fill an order for soup when she was a cashier and not the waitress. She had a quiet kindness to her and seemed to be going through the motions of her job but with much on her mind. He was happy to have a conversation with anyone now that he was in a new town. He loved how people had so many stories to tell. People were, after all, his life's work, and in that case it was fitting for him to love such a thing. He believed that one must love the work they do or should not do it at all.

The cashier responded to his request with a smile and quickly placed his order and directed him to a table to rest. He made direct eye contact with her and said a quick thank you. She smiled with a nod and went about her business.

Across from his table, he could see two men in the beginning stages of a serious conversation. One man, he noticed, was notably from India wearing his customary dress and the other of Asian descent. He could not help but see the headline of the newspaper that the men were discussing. The headline read, *Another Holy War*. His heart sank to the depths of an all-too-familiar sadness for the state of the world. He felt the prick of anguish for the human race that seemed to be dying like a grape on the vine of society.

Walking the dusty roads, he was often removed from the daily news, although it did not seem to change the fact that, to read it or not, he would absorb the truths of the world vicariously through overhearing the conversations of others. His

107

The Great Gathering of Gods Soul

mind and eyes were infiltrated by passing newsstands or radio broadcasts while passing through some remote city. The larger cities were inundated with the news, and he could not escape it if he tried. He believed that the streets were news briefs by themselves, as he must only walk down a busy street to watch the news happen.

"I don't understand this, the worst wars are always holy, you know?" the Indian man said, staring into the eyes of his friend. "Everyone believes in God, no? So, what's the problem?"

"It is because people believe that God can only represent one people. So, for this they fight and kill, for exclusivity on God. To own Gods ultimate power," chimed in his friend.

Satya was touched by the presence of mind of this gentleman and how he had explained so simply and clearly the state of the world in his own observation and how accurate he was.

Satya could not help but speak. "It is so simple," he said out loud as the cashier brought him his water and soup. He noticed her sweet and slight smile at him as she lowered his bowl of soup.

"Thank you," he said to her as she walked away. Then he turned to the men again who were now looking at him and eager to hear his thoughts on the matter.

"It is so simple and yet the world thinks that in order for something to have meaning, it must be complex."

The heads of the men nodded in approval to his words, so he continued, "The problem is clear, but because the world has added so many issues to the problem, the source can no longer be seen."

"The nations serve God with their ego and judgment on others," the Indian man said as he agitatedly thumbed the edges of the newspaper. Satya noticed his apparent anxiety over the matter and understood, as all endure injustice and suffering.

"I have heard it said before that he who serves God out of the fear of going to hell is in bondage and a slave. One who serves God to achieve the kingdom is seen only as a bargainer. My question is this," Satya said. "Does God want a slave or a

108

bargainer, or is he more like us? Is it love he is after? Is it the lack of that sort of love that is the root to our destructiveness?"

There was a quiet moment of thought, and then the Indian man said,

"We have plenty of questions, man. What is the answer?" He looked over at his friend whose head was nodding in agreement.

Satya was proud to be in the presence of such awareness. At that moment, a soft breeze blew through his hair, and the men next to him sighed in gratitude. The heat of the day had been parching. The men appeared to feel the sanctity of his visit and looked at him as though it was he who beckoned the wind to blow.

He said calmly, "All this chaos will not last forever, friends. Remember that and keep your faith in man. For they know not what they do, just as Jesus stated."

The men looked at one another and then politely said their goodbyes. He imagined that they would go off to their families and love them just a little bit more that day.

"Go safely," Satya said to the men, and they in return gave a smile and an honoring nod to him and then were gone.

He began to eat his food, and it tasted better than anything he could remember. All things tasted better when he had gone without food for a long period of time. He savored the flavor of the creamy risotto, the tomatoes finely chopped, the love that must have gone into removing the beans from their pod and the black pepper that excited his pallet. He thought of the Parmesan cheese and how it smelled like pineapple in its

pale golden rind. He felt refreshed while tasting the water that seemed to quench his thirst that was like a dried-up desert. He had traveled the entire day on the dusty road that ultimately led him into town.

He looked around the little café and out the windows to gaze at the people passing by and in his inner world thought to himself, *there is someone in this town who needs my help.* He had always trusted the roads that called him to his next mission. It was a religion to him, and in that process he had faith.

The Great Gathering of Gods Soul

As he ate, he began to read the events of the world in the newspaper left on the table by the men. Reading the paper was something he did not often do because he realized that these were real people having horrible things happen to them. People often forgot that what was being read in the paper, seen on television or heard on the radio was a reality of something that had happened to another human being, not just a fictitious, unfeeling, unreal character. The world had become so desensitized to the suffering of their neighbors. Technology and progress had replaced humanity in so many ways, yet in spite of that fact, he picked up the paper and took a spoonful of his soup. He flipped through the paper and had that feeling of wishing he could do more to help than he did. The paper was full of what life had become: War, serial rapists, serial killers, domestic violence, child abduction, fraud, pornography, hunger, lack of housing, riots, pickets, political corruption, slander, tax inflation, wealth, poverty, homelessness, prostitution, drugs, disease and terrorism.

It had gotten worse every day. He wondered often if man would ever realize that they have the power to manifest any and all that they wish? They had already proven that they could manifest suffering. Why would they not try happiness or peace? He did not understand.

He wiped his mouth with the napkin and laid down the newspaper for the next passer-by. As he stood up, he felt the same breeze bless his face as if to remind him of the phrase, "I AM." He said to himself, *I will not forget.* He took that moment to appreciate his life and the travels he had come to know as a way of life. Many could not live as he did without feeling the stress of where to lay their head at night. But with such faith in the process of his life, there was no need for fear. He knew that a spirit had no limits and therefore, nothing to fear. He lived a life of honor and respect and in return was given the same and in abundance. He appreciated his life and found peace and joy in helping others. In that moment with the breeze on his face, he contemplated his life and felt content.

All his life he had a gift of perception for happiness as well as pain. He could sense pain in a room or see it in a facial expression. If pain were near him, he could sense it. Happiness was easy to see, it was taking the time to notice the pain of others and comforting them that made Satya special. In conversations he would have with others, he did not map out their future as much as he saw the little things. Mostly, he saw what they were capable of and who they could become if they believed in themselves. He had hope for mankind. But mankind's pain had seemed to dominate human existence and because of that he had adjusted protecting his own soul from taking on the negative energies of others. He would help but not sacrifice his own well-being. His work could not continue if he were not clear and perfect channel of light himself.

He walked toward the cashier to pay for his lunch and knew at once her pain. He could see it in her eyes as he had always seen in the eyes, the soul and its thoughts. He felt heartache and the sense that a small child was involved. He could sense it with his entire being. The reading came to him as it always did. There was no question; it was just as he had felt and seen it. He pulled out the money from his coin purse and handed it to her. When she looked up at him, he smiled kindly at her with care. "He will come back," Satya said, looking deep into her eyes with reassurance.

She froze for a moment at the unsuspecting comment and then the truth brought her tears to the surface, and she cried. What he knew was confirmed. He could see and feel the wave of pain that hit her, and so he continued in a whisper as to not draw attention to her.

"He loves you. He is lost within himself, torn between being a boy and being a man. He will return in three days, and he will have worked out his demons between you and the child."

Satya reached out to touch her hands as quiet tears ran down her face.

"Thank you," she whispered through her tears.

The Great Gathering of Gods Soul

He nodded to her gently and said, "Thank you is unnecessary. It is our duty to help one another. Have faith and be happy." He let go of her hand and walked out onto the road once more. He felt her watching him as he walked off into the distance. She had the look of surprise at the unsuspecting kindness of this stranger, a stranger who gave and asked nothing in return. It was a rare thing in society to give without price or expectation. But to Satya, there was no other way.

He stepped onto the road and looked down at his feet encased in old, worn sandals. He had a fondness for the sandals that had shared his journey around the world in the effort to help mankind. His feet were dusty from the open road, but he didn't mind. He smiled as he looked at the open road ahead with anticipation of what would lie ahead. He looked upon his dirty feet as badges of honor. As he walked up the road, he felt the urge to veer to the right. *It is the proverbial fork in the road,* he laughed to himself. As always, he listened to the internal voice and did as it said, and so he veered to the right.

He walked slowly down the road passing by small houses in various stages of wear and tear and noticed the poverty-stricken homes. Each of the broken-down homes had a front door of stained glass that was beyond beauty, as if to speak of an ancient story of glorious days gone by—a time of the past that had long since been forgotten and taken over by scarcity. Perhaps a time before the world had realized the harsh realities of civilization: starvation, homelessness, and, worst of all, hopelessness—the evil of the world. He believed that all things became worse in the presence of hopelessness. His eyes were prisons, unable to flee from viewing the irony of such beauty mixed with poverty. He wondered on the kind of pain and hardship these people must go through.

Quite often, he himself went without food and drink, but it was his freedom and outlook on life that made even hunger a part of his adventure. The faith he had was enough to ensure that he would never go hungry for long. Even in the most trying times, he would continue on the path of service to others. Always, in some way, he was provided for or taken care of. For those things he had always been grateful. Those were, indeed, the provision for his life's work, and they were enough. His faith in the goodness of man always removed the obstacles set before him, and he had learned to see them as guidance and not blocks to his goal. He continued walking and observing.

He wondered if these people had children and how much harder it must be for a man's soul condition to watch his child suffer for the necessities of life. He only had himself to show concern for, although his work caused him to be overwhelmed with the feelings of suffering for others. Still, he was not a parent and could not fully understand their torment, but he tried. That much he understood.

He walked the dirt road until it became paved, and he heard the slight buzzing sound of a bustling city ahead. It was the busier side of town. He heard the sound of cars honking their horns in the distance. Inner warmth came over his body as it had always done when he came to a place of need. He knew that somewhere within that small city was someone in need of his healing. Kindness had always attracted those in need. Kindness was a commodity rarely shown in these troubled times. He lived in a world far too busy to be concerned with the welfare of the needy. The idea of welfare had long since gone away. The world produced so many ways to help the needy but those who were not needy became burdened with the taxes of charity. Eventually, the complaints of those who were not in need and in the office did away with all welfare. The world had succeeded in so many ways but compassion. Those who did not have family littered the streets as the homeless. There was no longer help for the needy other than from the churches and kind individuals. Kindness was still very much alive in society but was hard to find in the money-and progress-driven world.

The roads were paved but broken and old. The ancientness of Siena was mixed with the modern. Shiny new cars of futuristic design drove through the city, while others barely ran. Activists who were saving the world of pollution partially used solar cars that were used as a tribute to spare the

The Great Gathering of Gods Soul

air, and there were people on bicycles and scooters everywhere. For a moment he was reminded of the busyness of India.

The times spoke of old and new, and there were causes for everything, everywhere and visibly noticeable. Throughout the primordial city there stood erect, broken-down buildings next to extreme wealth. People who did not care for other human beings walked on the street next to religious fanatics who said they did. The world was in a deteriorating state savaged by crime, earthquakes, poverty and disease. The suffering was catastrophic. Men, women and children were begging aggressively on the streets and others were just sleeping out in the open and in entryways with signs that read "HELP ME." There were people on the streets that were dying and terminally ill with diseases and others with skin disorders that looked as though their skin was bubbling and peeling from their face. The homeless lay in the open streets because they had nowhere to go and nowhere to die. The stench of those who suffered filled the air, smelling of sickness and sweat that had not been cleansed for more days than could be numbered. Their breath was vile, and their bodies oozed a smell of death, as if trying to detoxify all that was impure from the tongues and pores of their skin. The rumbling moans of a decaying society and forgotten people were mixed with the laughter and joys of the active city. Yet, the city could not silence the cries that were scratching at the surface to remind people that humanity was still needed. Health insurance had gone away long ago for the poor, and most people just didn't care anymore. Caring souls were the minority and could only help so many. Those who didn't care outnumbered those who needed help.

Satya watched the fortunate in society pass by the starving and homeless as if they didn't even exist. Perhaps for some it was survival of the fittest. For others perhaps they did not want to help those who would take their money and use it for drugs or alcohol, or perhaps they just did not want to see the reality of the harsh world. Satya believed that despite the reason the homeless were in that decadent condition, they were in need for something more important; hope. Society had become so

The Great Gathering of Gods Soul

callous to the neediness of others, and from town to town, city-to-city, country-to-country it was the same — always the same.

As he continued walking through town, he came upon a mysterious-looking tavern of sorts and looked up to read the name of the building, *Gwo Ban Anj*. In English, underneath was the translation "Initiated Soul." A feeling came over him that beckoned him to enter the seemingly sacred place. This was the place to which he had been drawn.

He had no more money in his pocket, which was often the case, but that was of no concern to him. *God is here,* he uttered as he pushed open the heavy and somewhat out-of- place, Moroccan-looking doors and entered.

Inside, it was dark and lit by candles on chandeliers and tables. It had an atmosphere of unified worldliness and spirituality. There were yellow lights in every corner and at the tops of the ceilings. The walls were gold leaf, and the floors were made of hardwood. Beautiful wall tiles graced the backs of the tables. The most grand of all was the enormous Buddha statue that took up the entire side of the wall from the floor to the ceiling. The Buddha statue graced the dining area and entryway, and its size was breathtaking.

The tavern gave him the feeling of being in another world, a world of the exotic, of spirituality and acceptance. It was early yet and not yet filled to capacity. Satya noticed that every culture seemed to be accounted for and every sort of dress. He walked through the dining area and was not noticed at all. All were enjoying their meals and social engagement. He took in the enticing smell of cuisine and was grateful as he walked up the stairs to the bar. He found an empty chair at the bar and sat down on the stool. Within moments, the bartender came to take his order.

"May I have a glass of water, sir?" he asked.

The bartender obliged. Satya noticed a feeling of peace in the tavern and a feeling that all were welcome there — a place that seemed to have no cultural barriers or racial iniquity. It was rare for such a place to be in existence in the day of the almighty dollar. He was certain that the owners of the tavern must have

The Great Gathering of Gods Soul

some desire to make money, no doubt, but appeared to have the yin and yang in perfect alignment, and so it was seemingly successful and spiritual.

He found comfort there and although he knew he could not stay, he was happy to have found such a place to dwell in even for a short time. As he finished his water, he couldn't help but notice a room where people were entering and leaving that was hidden behind a thick red drape. Some would enter with offerings of fruit or flowers and exit the mysterious room behind the curtain with nothing in their hands. He had noticed some time earlier that a woman had entered the room, and although many others had come and gone since, she still remained. He wondered if it could be a sort of praying room. *Her troubles must be deep as she has been in there for quite some time,* he thought. He stood up and thanked the bartender for the water and made his way toward the thick red curtain to see what mystery lay behind the velvet barrier.

He stood before the veil and with his right hand slowly pulled the curtain open just enough for him to slip through sideways so not disturb anyone. What he saw took his breath; it was beautiful. A statue of Mother Mary stood in grace with her arms wide open as to receive the prayers of those who had come to her for rescue. Mother Mary, the mother of love and purity, silently waited to hear the prayers of those in need. The statue was made of solid white marble and was surrounded by fruit, flowers and various offerings. A golden veil adorned the statue, hanging from above her and draping down, behind and on all sides of her. It was glorious and cast an illuminant glow as if it were an aura of her compassion that could be seen to the human eye.

He too felt the silent comfort in that room where so many came to receive. Tea lights lit the room with soft and subtle lighting throughout, and lined the floor in front of the statue and on the various pieces of heavy wooden antique furniture that lured him in further.

He saw the woman whom he had noticed earlier kneeling before the statue deep in prayer. She seemed troubled by the

The Great Gathering of Gods Soul

look of intenseness on her face. He sensed she was sad, and she appeared like one who had been beaten by the world. Satya knelt down next to her on the rug in front of the statue and suddenly she opened her eyes to acknowledge his presence.

"Hello," he whispered quietly, to her, "Are you all right, miss?"

She looked at him briefly and did not answer. Ever so softly he said, "I am a healer of sorts and quite good at listening."

She looked at him and still said nothing, yet this time she managed a smile.

"I know you see me as a complete stranger," Satya said, "but the eyes are the imprints of the soul, and my soul is good. Look and see." He smiled down at her.

She slowly smiled back at him but still said nothing.

"I would love to talk with someone myself," Satya added. "I have been on a long journey in solitude with no one to relate to. Perhaps you could help me as well?"

He saw that the expression on her face had begun to soften.

"Sometimes the kindness of strangers can outweigh that of family. I know," he said. "I have seen it."

"What sort of healer?" she asked with curiosity.

"There are many ways to heal," he said. "Sometimes I lend my ear to listen. I believe sometimes people just need to be heard to release their pain."

He had her attention, and so she looked at him and listened intently. He continued, "Some need a physical healing of their body and only need be taught the secret healing method. For others, they need healing of their mind. Very often it is the workings of their own thoughts that make them ill. So, my dear lady, I am a healer of all sorts. What is it that you summoned me here for?"

Her eyes became large with surprise.

"What do you mean, *for what did I summon you here?* I have only just met you. I don't even know your name," she said defensively.

Satya expected such a reaction so with no change in his tone at all he responded softly in explanation, "I go where I am drawn to go. It was no mistake that I ended up here." He shook his head. "This is the way of my life. I feel and then I go to where the feelings grow stronger. It is a calling and today I was called to this place, at this very moment. I do not question it, friend, for I have faith in the process. So here I am."

He stopped speaking and looked at her with his gentle, comforting smile and could see the tenseness subside in her shoulders and face. A brief silence followed, which he was quite accustomed to as most people were startled briefly by his directness. It was not every day that such mystical conversations occurred in the ordinary life of others. Yet these kinds of conversations were the only kind that Satya ever had, for he was mystical and could have it no other way.

She tucked her hair behind her ears and swallowed the lump in her throat as if it were hard for her to speak the words she wanted to say. Satya saw her inner struggle and found that asking a question often opened the doorway to the flow of communication.

"What is it that makes you so sad?" he asked, knowing that her pain was deep and waiting on the edge of discovery.

Her head dropped down to her chest and tears began to flow freely. It was a deep pain that came from the soul. She sobbed with her head in her hands. When she caught her breath and looked up, she said, "I have lost a child." Tears streamed from her eyes. He could see that it was not only the loss of the child but her hurt feelings at God for this tragedy that tormented her. The tears she shed were that of a spiritual cry. She was understandably and mistakenly wounded by the misunderstanding that it was God who allowed this to happen. It was God who took the blame. It was always God who took the blame. Satya leaned his head closer and looked into her eyes to let her know that he cared to listen to her.

"I can't stop crying. I don't understand why God has allowed this to happen to my baby; why he allowed my child to not have the life he was promised." Satya heard the depths of

The Great Gathering of Gods Soul

her despair. "I am so sad all the time. I can't function. I want to die," she said, sounding hopeless. "I don't know how to survive my child's death. Perhaps, it will be the death of me also?"

"Give me your hands," he said. She did as he asked. "You do not understand the journey of the soul and so you are hurt. This child is not lost to you. I know the ancient tales of wisdom in regard to the travels of the soul and so I will share it with you. This is what I know and live by. It is said that it is quite common that a soul who enters life for the first time in the body finds it constricting, and so it decides it is not ready and pulls its life force from its fleshy body. Perhaps, your baby's soul was not ready to enter this planet of hardship and suffering so it withdrew. But this I know. The child is promised to you and will come again to enter your life for a purpose. For all life forms come with a purpose."

"How can you be sure?" she said.

He took her hands into his and turned them face up. "Close your eyes," he said, and she did. He took his index finger and ran it down her palm. When he finished, he said, "Open your eyes." She opened her eyes, and he asked her, "What did I do just now?"

She looked at her hand and said, "You ran your finger down my palm."

"How do you know?" he asked her.

"I felt it," she replied.

"This is how I know about your baby's sweet return. I felt it," he answered her simply.

He continued when he saw the sparkle in her eye. He knew that look for he had seen it before. It was hope.

"The child cannot come again into a life with you unless you are able to care for it. This child needs a sturdy mother to help him accomplish his purpose in life. He will do great things. The child waits for you, so today I came to deliver this message to you. That is all I know."

The woman sat and listened to him, and he could see from her face that the well of water pouring from her eyes had dried up. In such a short time, her faith and hope had been restored. He could feel her spirit strengthen in the presence of knowingness, and it made him feel worthy and humble for this gift that he had been given.

With a smile of success on Satya's face, he could see that the woman noticeably felt relieved. She took a deep breath and it looked to him as though she had released the shadow in her heart.

"You are free now with your hope and faith restored," he said. "There is more for you to learn as it is not enough for me to heal you, but you must learn to heal your own soul as you will need this ability throughout your life."

"I want to learn," she said.

He patted her folded hands that lay on her thighs in seated meditation and began, "You must learn the secret of healing. It is the only way to ensure that this does not happen again, this depression and loss of faith," he said.

With a nod from her, he continued teaching. "I will tell you this secret and in doing so it will change your life. It is a truth that is so simplistic that most never absorb its profundity and therefore never apply it to their life."

He could see the woman waited in anticipation for this life-altering teaching he was promising to tell.

"Your body has within it the ability to heal itself and every ailment that enters it, physically and emotionally. But the lack of our own knowingness to this truth blocks our ability to use it and in so doing, blocks our ability to heal ourselves. Because we do not believe that we can heal ourselves and even worse, we give our power up to others who proclaim they can instead, we do not acknowledge our ability. This is not isolated to just healing. It is in everything we do in life and in everything we believe we can or cannot do. Even our speech, *I think, maybe, I'll try, I'll ask, I should.* All these passive words say to us that we do not have the power to decide. The truth is that we decide who we are and who we want to become. We manifest that which we think and believe in our own hearts. That, my dear, is the secret. If we have no hope, we manifest hopelessness. Do you understand?"

120

The Great Gathering of Gods Soul

"Yes, please continue."

"Your sadness and lack of hope only led you to more of the same since the energy you create is yours and will always come back to its creator. You are free now and so you must apply this truth so that you do not fall prey to its trickery again." He gazed deeply in her eyes to be sure she understood.

The woman seemed to hear the ring of truth in his words and was growing stronger by the moment. Her demeanor had changed from that of a weak and solemn spirit to one filled with hope for the future and eager to apply and remember the things he was saying to her.

"You are so wise."

He smiled at her and said, "Life is but an awakening to ancient knowledge that must be earned again and unlocked in each life. It is there all along, and for the enlightened ones, it is their sword of victory for the battle of survival and suffering so prevalent on this planet. I am an old soul who has lived many lives."

She nodded, as she understood a life of suffering herself. He could see the light in her eyes and knew their time was coming to an end.

"Knowingness dissolves all untruths. You will move forward now. Never forget this day," he said as he stood up to leave. She quickly reached over to hug him in gratitude.

"You will be fine now. Do not worry, okay? You are strong. Now go and live a good life. One that you choose. What you do not understand in the future, ask and your teacher will appear."

As he said that last line, he walked toward the curtain, and before walking through it, he looked back at her with his sweet half smile and said goodbye. The curtain fell behind him and he was gone. As Satya exited the Gwo bon Anj, he felt the crisp fresh air on his face and took it in and smiled. He was blessed with the feeling of humility and gratitude for the ability to help others who were lost. He was a life map to so many who were lost, and it gave his life meaning and purpose to help them.

He had no idea where he was going now. He enjoyed moments of grace to relax and think only of himself. They were few and far in between. The sun was going down, and in the direction that he was walking, he spotted a small park.

"Ah, a place to sleep," he said quietly to himself as he hurried toward it. Shops were closing their doors and nightspots were just opening. The homeless were still in all the same places he had seen them in earlier and many more had migrated in the same direction. Many homeless were pushing their carts full of their belongings. The elite insane, in another time, would have been in a hospital if that were something that was still paid for by the state. There were two types of life—those who thrived and those who were walking dead, for whom no one cared. He had no fear of mixing with such individuals. He was also homeless and to him it was an adventure and opportunity to help. For helping was what he lived for.

The lights of the park were turned on as the sun began its descent and Satya found a bench to sit on. He contemplated on the young woman and savored his joy that he could help her. Suddenly, a man with food came and sat on the bench and opened his Styrofoam container and sighed, "AHHHH, at last we meet." Satya could not help but laugh and in doing so got the man's attention. The man gave a smile to Satya. He could smell the aroma of roasted peppers and beef and looked over to see what it was. The man eating noticed his glance and smiled at him again.

"Ah, yes," Satya said. "Roasted root vegetables and marinated pork ribs is a fine meal." At that, the man tore off the lid of his foam container and filled it with some of his roasted vegetables and meat.

"Then you will eat, too," the man joyfully replied as he handed Satya the food in the lid and the plastic spoon that he was not using. Satya was pleased at the man's pleasantness and generosity.

"Thank you, kind sir. I am hungry, so you have come at the right time."

"Eat, drink and be merry, right?" the man said.

122

"Indeed," Satya said with a smile that showed his gratitude. They concentrated on eating and watching passers-by and when the man finished his food, he got up to leave.

"Thank you, sir," Satya said to the generous man. The man just looked at him and smiled as if to say, *no problem.*

The sun was almost fully set in the night sky, and it was one of his most favorite times. The setting of the sun uncovers the moon, which has been there hiding all along. He made the parallel to that of man's awareness and how it too is there all along waiting to be uncovered.

He found a safe spot by a tree that would be his bed for the night and lay down on his back to look up at the sky. He pondered the wisdom of the tree and always felt safe next to something so ancient that had survived the ages. *If the tree could only talk*, he thought to himself. *What a companion it would be-- so ancient and timeless.* Perhaps that is why he had felt so at home next to it and under the stars. Many nights, he slept under the trees and shining lights.

Chapter Nine

Undici

Another day in Siena continued the next morning and during that time he saw many places and visited the people. There were many who seemed to need his help and healing and he noticed how so many people only needed to be heard and have their anguish listened to. They would show him their kindness in return for his deeds, by giving him food, drink, and a place to bathe. Many times, they would even invite him to stay in their homes providing his shelter. As was usually the case, he gained notoriety in a quiet and humble way. He became well known for his healing and comforting ability.

Later that day, while walking along the busy streets observing the people shopping and interacting with others, he noticed a young woman walking closely behind him. She stopped and hid here and there, to not be noticed by him. But being aware of his surroundings, he could feel someone in need and so he turned to see her hiding behind a clothes rack that was in front of a small, recycled clothing store called *Undici*.

He looked her in the eyes as she hid behind the clothes. Because it was obvious that he could see her and that she was hiding, he walked to her calmly.

"What is it that you are in need of, dear?" he said gently and with an extended hand to her, inviting her to come out from behind the clothes. She was timid and seemed a little frightened at being caught. She said nothing in reply to his question, so he spoke again.

"Go ahead, speak. You know who I am. I am kind and will listen." Saying nothing else, he looked at her with a soft smile and showed patience.

"I have been sent to find you, kind sir. I apologize for my behavior, but I am not accustomed to approaching strangers on the streets. Please forgive me."

With an initial look of concern, he then smiled. "Of course, it was not my first time being followed, I imagine it will not be my last," he said with sincerity showing no distress. Yet her serious demeanor remained unchanged, and it was then that he saw the deep circles of trouble beneath her eyes.

Moving closer to her and reaching for her hands he spoke to her.

"What troubles you, young one?" he asked, reaching out for her hand. She responded by allowing him to hold her right hand and they stared at one another for a moment. She was merely the age that he was when he left Manzanillo. Her hair was straight and dark brown, shining in the sun, and her eyes were the color of green olives.

The streets were busy with people shopping and performing their daily routines. The various street merchants were everywhere selling a plethora of goods, while the street people hovered to steal what they could when no one was watching. The market was filled with joy and anxiety for the love of food and the annoyance for those no one cared about. Despite the busyness of the streets and the noise of the people, cars and bike bells, the girl had the look of intensity as though there were no one else but him standing before her. Feeling her discomfort, he was eager to help her, and his concern showed on his face. He could see by her expression that she wanted to tell him, but she hesitated and possibly was even scared to reveal her dilemma. He had seen it before; the way people were afraid to speak the truth out of fear of being judged by others. Many people seemed to only want to have their ears tickled, hear the things they wanted to hear, when that was the last thing they needed. He believed that love was an ability to tell people what they needed to hear, not what they wanted to hear. He had learned that valuable truth through Asha and Ke'ren and had never forgotten it. So, to encourage her to communicate, he moved in closer to protect her secret from prying ears.

"I know no other way to say this, kind sir, other than to just say it. There is something, a strange activity, a feeling," she said looking down as though she were experiencing the remembrance of fear and distress while she spoke the words to him. "My mother sent me to find you because it is ruining her businesses and the employees are nervous, and there is so much turmoil. Even the shop renters are not paying their rent on time or at all. Things are constantly breaking and going wrong. My mother sent me to find you because she heard of your calmness, foresight and healing ability. The news of you has traveled fast on these streets of Siena. Mother thought that perhaps you could use your ability of sight to help see what was happening to her businesses?"

He took a moment of silence because while she spoke of her mother, it was as though her mother were standing next to her. He could sense the mother and her intentions, but he said nothing. He just stared at the girl on the street of the market while he saw her mother as if in a dream, sitting at her desk. He felt her love for money and felt her ill will to others. She was numb like a machine. He stood there silently before the girl while he saw his vision but said nothing of it to the girl because it was not pleasant.

"Do you think I am crazy?" she asked.

"No, do not take my silence for disbelief. I am more aware of the spirit realm than you can know," he said looking at her in somewhat of a deep gaze from the vision he had just seen. "My name is Satya, young lady. What is yours?" he asked, bowing his head slightly to her and holding his hands in a prayer position.

"My name is Barissa. My family has owned land in Siena for generations and it now belongs to my mother. It used to be one of the finest vineyards and gardens in Siena, but now it is on Verona Street. Do you know it?" she asked.

"No, I am sorry. That is one street I have not yet walked down," he said and smiled. As they stood there on the cobblestone sidewalk in front of the old clothing store the people passed them by, disinterested in their conversation.

"Where is this Verona Street, young miss?" he asked.

"It is a few streets over. I can take you there if you like?" she asked him.

"As it turns out, I am doing nothing at the moment," he said with a mesmerizing smile. She smiled in return and made a gesture for them to begin their stroll to lofty Verona Street. The hair on his arms and on the back of his neck stood up as they got closer and he could feel the vibration of active turbulence, not of this world. As they headed in the direction she led him, his body heat increased to a burning temperature from the inside out and he knew something was terribly wrong. It was normal for him to feel warmth but not this anxious feeling with which it was coupled.

On the way, they had pleasant conversation and talked little about the concern at hand that sent her out into the streets to find him. When they arrived at the entrance of her property it looked as if it were a palace. There were roses in full bloom, covertly acting as shields to the mansion. An intercom was placed at the huge gate so that no one unwanted could enter.

Barissa dialed a code and the gate opened for them and they began the long walk to approach the front entrance up the paved road. As they walked slightly uphill he looked around and saw the beauty of the garden that lined the small road. The garden was vast, and he gazed out upon its loveliness and yet he was filled with a chaotic energy like that of static. He stopped in his track, feeling dizzy, and his stomach suddenly turned with nausea. When that moment passed vibrations came up to his throat and a word came to his lips that he could not resist. "Oscurita," he said in his deep voice.

"Why did you say that?" Barissa asked in an eerie whisper with eyes large like someone who had seen death.

"It came to my lips, and I could not withhold what was given to me. Clearly it was meant for this house to hear. Is it Italian because I do not know what it means? What is it that I said?" Satya asked her as she turned and began walking again toward the huge door leading into the estate. Lost deep in thought, he walked with her waiting for her to reply.

"It means 'Darkness,' Sir," she said solemnly, and with the same sense of discomfort he felt from her at their first meeting moments before. He sensed that the girl knew the darkness that had dwelt within their home for some time. Suddenly, the lushness did not look so beautiful to him because he could see with his mind's eye and all the magnificence displayed could not hide the ugliness within. There was darkness in that house-in the soul of that house. And poor Barissa was aware of and caught in the middle.

The huge doors opened wide with a mere touch of her hand and the house seemed to invite them into their purgatory. Cast iron furniture, solid and heavy, filled the home and the most beautiful of Italian décor surrounded the home that appeared to be very old.

"How long have you lived in this house?" Satya asked her.

"All my life, Sir, but it has been in my family for three generations. Just like the land that used to surround this house. Only now, it is gone," she said looking down. "Just like my mother," and then looked up at him. "I mean, my mother is here, Sir, but it is like she is gone because she is so withdrawn into running the profit machine."

Satya tilted his neck and asked, "What is the profit machine, if you don't mind me asking?"

"It is what she calls this land. She tore down what had been in our family for all this time and said that it could be a profit machine if real estate were built onto the land where our ancestors sweat all their life to keep as vineyards and tomato gardens."

"And you think she was wrong for doing this?" he asked, reading into her tone.

"I knew nothing of such things when it occurred. I was just a child," she replied to him not answering his question.

"Yes, but do you think it was wrong?" he asked again, trying to gaze into her eyes.

"They do," she said as her face turned pale and the circles under her eyes grew dark. She began to lead him down the hall to what he believed was the location of her mother. His skin turned hot and flushed his face. Something was wrong in the home, and it felt strong in the house. There was a sinister feeling as though they were not alone. While walking down the hall he felt the presence of something following beside and behind him, but he said nothing, and just kept moving.

The Great Gathering of Gods Soul

Finally, they came to a large office door and the door opened from the inside. A maidservant exited quickly looking into Satya's eyes briefly and then down again as she left the room, rushing passed him. It was cold inside with no feeling of warmth that a home should give off. Nevertheless, the house was lovely to look at. The house was filled with designer furniture, window treatments, expensive carpets, chandeliers and plenty of sunlight entering into the home. But as nice as it was, he knew that things were not always what they seemed. Some things were mere mirages, smoke and mirrors, and the truth wasn't truth at all. It was only the appearance of what someone wanted others to believe was truth. There was something going on in the house that wasn't right. It was a feeling of anxiety or tension that was unexplainable.

Barissa held the door open, and he could smell the scent of fresh roses that came from the side table full of white roses by the entrance of the room. When he looked in he saw a lovely older woman sitting in her chair with her desk buried in papers. She was elegant and had the look of a woman who was mild-tempered and soft spoken. But when she stood up to greet him, her voice did not seem to match the image that he had created in his mind. Her voice was hard and when she smiled he saw the beauty of her face but heard the voice of a gasping songbird trapped inside the weeds that had grown within her soul. He sensed her and knew she was an abyss of secret thoughts full of the ugliness of her choices.

"Yes, you are the man I sent Barissa out for. I require your assistance. How much for your services?" she asked and smiled.

A little surprised by her abruptness and total lack of formal introductions, he looked at Barissa who, to him, could have been born of another mother. They had no similarity in etiquette style at all. Barissa was polite, kind and soft like a piece of cotton or a fragile butterfly. So, he looked at Barissa and she quickly chimed in, to introduce them.

"Mother, this is Satya. Satya, this is my mother, Vittoria."

Although Satya preferred to take a silent, somewhat passive approach, he felt uneasy in her presence and wondered

129

if he would be able to be subtle with the woman. She was abrasive and confrontational.

Satya extended his hand to her, and she took it. He kissed the back of her hand and her face looked surprised at his manners.

"My name is Satya, it is nice to meet you, Vittoria," he said with an honoring glance and soft-spoken voice.

She smiled at him and walked back around to her desk and pointed at the chair for him to take a seat.

"I hear you are a psychic."

"No," Satya said humbly, looking down with a grin. He had heard that so many times and never liked the sound of it. It was such a commercial title for a description of a gift that he believed all human beings possessed. Intuitiveness was a common commodity covered by centuries of layers and numbness. It wasn't psychic at all to him, but a primitive art. It was an art of listening. Listening had become something that people were allergic to doing in the modern era of technology. People had become less important because machines could replace them, and people constantly struggled to survive and stay good enough to keep their jobs. It was the same in every country; humans were competing with machinery.

"My daughter has told you why I have sent for you?" she asked.

"Yes Ma'am," he replied. "But I perform no services," he added mildly and sincerely.

"What is your background?" she said with a somewhat judgmental voice, trying to define a category or class to put him in. He understood her right away, by her covert methods and manipulations. He had lived through such strategies all his younger years as a child and knew them well. Vittoria possessed the same negative undercurrent as his mother had, but the sight of her was deceiving. It reminded him of a scripture that he had learned as a boy growing up in Manzanillo surrounded by Catholics. It said that Evil itself was always transforming into an angel of light. He laughed to himself with that knowledge because the knowingness of that truth removed any mystery in man's motives. He had the ability to recognize people's thoughts and internal wars within themselves. Perhaps that was what made him the best candidate for such troubles and troubled people, he contemplated to himself.

Because of her ways, he knew the tone he would have to take with her. "My dear Vittoria," he said with a slight smile and laughter, "I am no one to you or anyone. I have no services to render, nor do I seek material gain. I have no category in which you can place me in because I am no one and nothing. Yet I am everyone and everywhere. I am flesh and blood, seeking peace and sharing it with all whom will listen."

Curious, she leaned back in her chair listening to him and tapping her pen on her income ledger. Behind her was a giant window bestowing the view of bushels of assorted flowers and the distant grass that seemed to extend quite a distance. It appeared that she did not know what to say. Money was clearly a manipulating force to her, and he understood that she had used money as a form of control on those who had none. Her ways were obvious to him by her demeanor, the feeling of power she projected and her display of wealth. She was a suppressive person.

It was the same way everywhere when it came to money. People had the same false sense of power that money would bring to those who felt powerless otherwise. He was amazed by the concept of power because it appeared to him that power only existed if the masses supported the concept of money equaling power. He never understood money equaling the idea of being better, even as a child he thought it seemed backwards. To him, he perceived that the servant was actually the master, so he never felt any different around money or poverty. It seemed to him that the servant had the advantage because he was not a slave to money or greed and therefore did not struggle to keep it. At least the servant was free. Money did not impress him nor did poverty scare him. He knew money did not make a person of greater or lesser value. Nor did it make them greater or lesser human being. There was only nothingness and sameness to him. His indifference to having, or not having, was the key to his happy life. He focused on what goodness lay inside and the rest always seemed to be added to him as needed.

He understood that Vittoria was a businesswoman, and now he sat before her, a man who placed no value on the currency she used to dominate others. She could not use money to control him, and he quickly saw that it was the only thing that gave her power.

"What is it that you are in need of Vittoria?" he said politely.

With a slight discomfort at appearing needy to her daughter, she replied.

"Barissa, please leave."

She was abrupt to her daughter and never once took her eyes off Satya. Barissa was still standing at the door where they had entered, looking appalled at her mother's rudeness. Rolling her eyes, Barissa then looked at Satya as if she were apologizing for her mother's behavior and walked out letting the heavy door slam shut behind her.

"I own all this land and have built business buildings on it and rented them out. I also own several stores myself. I own a bakery, deli, and a few restaurants in town. I need for nothing," she said.

"Then why am I here?" he asked. "Surely you need something?"

Her eyes squinted for a moment as though the thought of needing something or someone was detestable. Still, he knew he was there for a reason of need and so he said what he believed she needed to hear. Still, it appeared her pride did not allow her to respond to his question, so he began to speak again, "You know, I have been all over this earth, Vittoria and have seen many different types of people, different cultures of political and financial standing. Yet, with all the differences, I have found that people can be so independent that their total lack of need for anything isolates them from the joy of loving or having someone to share their life with. The cycle of life is change and interacting with people. There is a constant toss up, going from good to bad on a continuum. People are the buffers to life's misfortunes and

132

if you do not share them with someone, you bear the weight of life's hardships alone. It is unnecessary to live life that way. The joy in life is to share it. To not need anything is not always a good thing," he said, engaging her.

"What school did you go to Satya," she said condescendingly, ignoring the depth of what he had said.

Quickly, he responded to her, knowing her intention was not sincere, but to deflate any knowledge he had on the subject.

"The University of Life, madam," he said. "What I have learned in my travel throughout the world, you cannot get in a book, nor can it be bought. If we place value on or believe that learning is valid only through traditional venues, then I am afraid I know nothing. And the prophets, philosophers, mystics and poets throughout History who had no formal training, also knew nothing. Each path takes its own road and no matter where the turn, it was meant to be. 'Maktub.' He said looking at her.

"What is Maktub?" she asked.

"It is something that I always remember in times of need and in times of faith. It means, 'It is written.' We choose a path. We have an option to choose one of two paths that are written. Either we chase our dreams or watch them pass. In either event, we learn the same lessons. Whether it is through regret or through the joy of living, we learn it regardless because the same lesson occurs over and over again until we get it. Things happen as they were meant," he said.

She sighed with slight irritation as Satya stood up from his seat and came walking toward her. Heading toward the window behind her, he smiled, passed her and came face to face with the view beyond the window. "I would like to walk through that garden. Please?" he asked her.

"Fine," she said. "I'll get a servant to take you." She stood up from her desk chair.

"No, I would like you to show me the garden. We have things to discuss," he said boldly. The stunned look on her face did not surprise him nor did she protest. He was there for a purpose, and he was not going to let her pride interfere. She needed something and he sensed that her inability to control him with money or power made her uneasy. He knew that she would not ask for help now that he did not acknowledge her power.

"I will need to change," she said, looking down at her business attire. "I am not dressed for the garden," she added softening her tone.

"Of course," he said with no sense of hurry. "I will wait for her at this window," He turned to gaze out again. He felt such a calmness looking out at the garden, and he wondered to himself when the last time was that she had been in the presence of life in the garden.

She left the room and as he looked out, he reminisced how he used to look out from the monastery in Bhutan. The beauty of the garden brought back memories of the rice fields and of Yava. The thought and vision of him and the fields brought pure joy to him in that moment. Then he thought of Asha and Ke'ren, thinking how he would need their guidance to help this woman. She was hardened by the world and her negative energy made him want to flee. Perhaps the nerve she hit in him was that she was so similar to his own mother? But he was conscious of that fact and was working to maintain his reactions and have patience with her. Still, silently to himself, he asked Ke'ren and Asha to be with his spirit and to offer any guidance they could offer. He thought to himself, *I am the Universe, and the universe is me. Give me all your patience.* He knew that Asha and Ke'ren heard his request and he felt happy to be part of the universe. He continued to look out the window, admiring the butterflies that were fluttering around as if they were dancing.

The Great Gathering of Gods Soul

Chapter Ten

Oscurita (Darkness)

The door of the office opened. "I am ready to go," Vittoria said abruptly as she looked at him from beneath an oversized straw hat. Satya turned toward her and away from the window and simultaneously took a deep breath. He knew his request for patience had gone out just in time. He had an inkling that Vittoria was going to be a challenging project. As they walked out of the office she took him down a long hallway where he admired the Italian architecture and the intellectual feeling the house gave him. Bookshelves lined the halls and staircases, filled with the knowledge of the world that he felt such a love for. He knew that books had the power to bring the vastness of the world into a home without ever stepping out of comfort's door. Books had always held a special place in his heart for that very reason. They were his salvation and hope as a child, knowing that other worlds existed, and growth was possible. He wondered what part the books played in Vittoria's life. He wondered, because she had enough affection and love for knowledge, to store the books so nicely.

But it did not seem that Vittoria was living at all because she appeared caught in the motion of life without feeling the joys or the sorrows. She seemed numb to him and that was the worst of all foes. Emotion had to be present in order to evoke change. As they continued to walk down the wide and open walkway it began to lead to the back of the house where the light became bright once more. They eventually came upon two immense glass doors opening into the magnificent and blooming landscape. As the doors swung open, Vittoria let out a choking gasp the way an infant would when flushed with a sudden burst of air to the face. But as Satya looked at her, he could see it was not a traumatizing gasp, but one of bliss. He realized then that it must have been ages since she had enjoyed the luster of her own garden. Such a wonderful garden and home that had been in her family for ages, yet it was that same garden and home that was the cause of all her problems.

As they walked outside he felt the warmth of the sun and the instant beads of sweat it caused. Although it was hot, it was comfortable with the slightest sensation of a breeze. He could understand why such a pristine woman would want to stay inside. Sweating was not something she, as a rich businesswoman, would be accustomed to. Satya knew, however, that she needed grounding and centering herself to something other than her ledgers, café, deli or restaurants. She was wrapped up in a world of torment that she chose, sacrificing family and historic loyalty for profit. Perhaps it was to fill the coldness in her soul. The same coldness he sensed when Barissa described her mother to him in the market.

"Do you read the books on the shelves we passed?" he asked her.

"When I was a child and had time for mindless pursuits, I was able to read," she said. "Now I run the businesses and raise my daughter and she costs money."

"So, you slave for her then," Satya said bluntly. The look of shock and disdain was apparent on her face.

"I am not a slave to anything, sir. I love what I do, and I love my lifestyle."

"Do you?" he asked. "You do not appear happy to me." He said softly while walking past her, looking at the sharp prickly bushes, touching the satin smooth leaves of the tree's and smelling the sweetness of the flowers. When she remained speechless, Satya asked her, "What is it that you sent Barissa after me for, if you don't mind me asking, Vittoria?"

She was noticeably angry for being in his presence and stuck in the garden with him, yet she remained polite. She refused to reveal the answer or appear to need him for anything. "I don't need anything from you."

"Madam, am I to believe that you sent your only daughter into the market to fetch a complete stranger for no reason at all? We both know that would be absurd and a lie. So, might we get to the matter at hand? There is something happening in this

The Great Gathering of Gods Soul

house, I can feel it. Your daughter can also. She hears the voices. So, speak your truth and do it now, or I shall leave to visit others who are not ashamed or afraid to reveal their troubles and ask for help," he said with curtness and impatience. "I have no more time to play slap and tickle with you."

Forced to reveal her trouble she blurted out. "Okay. My daughter hears voices in the house. She is sane and so I do not understand what is happening to her. All hell is breaking loose in our home and in my businesses. I have all the money in the world but the constant problems that arise are overwhelming me. The amount of time and resources to find the help to do it seems to be overpowering the businesses themselves. I am exhausted," she said with a sudden look of release on her face. It was as though the choking pride lodged in her throat had been anointed with oil. Taking a deep breath, she touched the leaf of the rose in front of her and Satya began to turn around looking at all the flowers.

"Do you think that these flowers in this garden worry?" he asked her.

"Of course, they don't," she replied.

"And yet you and I both know that without water from others they will die in this garden. Still, they do not worry that their life relies primarily on another source besides their own."

"That's true," she replied, with creased brows. "What is that supposed to mean, Satya?"

"What it means is that despite the life and death issue the garden faces on a daily basis, it doesn't worry. With no brains at all, it has learned to face that which is out of its control and live in the moment and enjoy the harmony in its presence." By the look in her eyes, he could see that she understood some of his logic of living in the moment without fear.

"I have heard of the riddles in which you speak," she said with a chuckle to herself.

"Yes," he said and smiled." I suppose that you have. Yet the answer for you is to realize that there is no problem. There is only what is and there is only the present moment. There is only a problem when we deny living in the present moment and deny

The Great Gathering of Gods Soul

appreciating what we have been given, no matter what that is. Deny equals attack, and when we deny our job, our house, people, love or help, that which we deny, attacks us."

"I don't understand what you are saying to me. How can things attack me?"

"Tell me more of what is happening in your businesses," he asked her. "This will help me to apply this information to your life."

"Well, random things really," she said. "Things are breaking down when they showed no symptoms of wear, such as the stoves in the bakery, plumbing, and office equipment. Shipments for the bakery or restaurants not showing up, being short-staffed all the time, employees fighting and back stabbing, a high turnover in all of my establishments, and the commercial buildings I rent out have similar problems. Things occur with the renters that cause them to be late with rent payments or the building just falls apart for no apparent reason. I have even lost tenants from the voices and the mysterious things they say they see and hear."

Satya took a deep breath while touching the Acacia tree and looking up at its twisted branches. Its white blossoms silhouetted against the sky that had suddenly become overcast and dreary. A fast breeze whipped through the garden and Satya felt an eerie chill.

"What was that?" Vittoria said as the breeze went through the garden without warning.

"A message," he said. "You deny this land and the love your ancestors had for it."

"What are you talking about? I don't deny this land. I put a lot of money into this profit machine. My ancestors failed to see this land for the profitable resources. They were stupid, even with all those books.

"I built businesses that could produce more money than the gardens and vineyards were bringing. How many olives or tomatoes can you grow?" she asked sarcastically. "I was sick of the family business. It was time to move into the century and make some real money."

"So is it working," Satya said in response to her ugly, materialistic point of view.

"YOU SEE MY WEALTH DON'T YOU?" she said, spreading her arms out with the utmost haughtiness.

"Oh yes," he said calmly. "I see your wealth. I also see that you have lost touch with your daughter. I see that she loves you but does not like you. I see you in a house full of things but without love. I see you denying your heritage, your family and people in general."

Her eyes became like daggers, and judging from her silence, he gathered that she was stunned, never having anyone talk to her in that manner.

"I am sorry that I must say this to you, Vittoria. But part of caring for someone is telling them what they need to hear, not what they want to hear," he said apologetically.

She took the hit of his words to her heart and sat on the bench in the garden where they were. Perhaps she could not fight his words because deep down she knew they were true. She sat there looking as if she were reminiscing about unpleasant memories.

"The commercial buildings almost didn't happen," she said and then looked up at Satya. "During the construction of building, the land was flooded with water from a broken main line. The land was saturated. I stopped the construction long enough to let the land dry out but then I kept on with my plan and eventually the builders were able to finish the project. But things constantly broke down, even then."

"Your ancestors gave you a sign and you ignored it."

"What?" she said.

"The water was your sign to stop building. Didn't you have any doubts at that time whether or not you should be plowing down your family history and lifetimes of their work for your own selfish desires," he asked her.

"Yes, for a moment," she said, shrugging.

"Well, that was your sign to stop. Why did you ignore it?" he questioned her.

"Because I knew what I wanted, and nothing was going to stop me since I was given the deed to the land."

"Why do you disregard the signs, Vittoria?"

"My family warned me also not to do it. But I am in business to make money, Satya. I am not a mystic like you traveling the world to be free and serve others," she said sarcastically.

"Well, maybe you should be," he said in return. Then the conversation dropped off to nothingness and the feeling that he got from her stare was one of contemplation, rather than insult. They did not say another word as they began to walk again through the garden quietly. They admired the many flowers and heard the buzzing of the bees around them, felt the fullness of the bushes, touched the ridges of the trunks of the trees and listened to the melody of the fountains water and felt the peacefulness of the garden.

The greater part of the day had been spent in conversation and as they entered back into the house, Vittoria spoke again.

"Satya," she said so nicely that it surprised him. He looked at her and felt the warm feeling of happiness that one gets in the presence of a dear friend.

"Yes?" he replied gently.

"I would like to ask you to stay for dinner, if you have no pressing plans or others to attend to," she asked politely as though he were a friend that she respected.

Her voice had shifted from that of a cold woman who was only interested in business and herself to one of someone being a bit more open to his ideas. He sensed that it was his comment on the lack of relationship she had with her daughter and family that caused her to wonder if some of what he had been saying was true.

"I would love to stay for dinner," he said and bowed his head in respect as he had become accustomed to doing in Asia.

"I do have a few things to do before I end my day, but I would like for you to be comfortable. We have many rooms here, so it is no trouble to give you one to rest in or freshen up in before dinner. "Would that be all right with you?"

"Yes," he said bowing his head again. "That would be wonderful." Barissa was called and arrived as Vittoria went off in the other direction. Barissa happily showed him to a room where he showered and lay refreshed on the comfortable bed top and took a small nap. When he woke, he could see that the sun had gone down almost completely, and he felt as though it were a new day. He had always felt that way after a rest. He woke to the pleasant mood of knowing that he made a difference in someone's life. He had helped to cause another human being to awaken from her comatose submission to the world's way of doing things.

He felt as though he helped reach Vittoria somehow, yet he did not know for sure what words in specific that changed her shift, and he didn't care. He only felt the joy of knowing that she was thinking about things that had laid dormant for many years and that she had felt grateful enough to want more of his company.

As he sat up in the bed, a light tap on the door occurred. He quickly rose to his feet to open the door. It was Barissa, dressed in a soft flowery dress, and smiling at him.

"It's time for dinner, Satya. By the way, I don't know what you said to mother, but she seems so calm and peaceful. She invited the whole family over for a feast and she hasn't been around the family for years," she said with glee. "Whatever you did Satya, you are a miracle worker. Thank you for showing me my mother again," she said, and he saw the shine of light in her eyes and knew it was a sign of happy tears. He knew then how much she had missed her mother's spirit and how healing it was for Barissa to see it in her again.

He smiled, touching her cheek, and she led him to the dining room palace. When they entered through the lathe of drapes, separating the dining room from the others, he was taken aback by how many people were standing with glass in hand to cheer him. "So, this is the one who brought us back together again," a man in the crowd said with a smile and joyful demeanor.

Satya just stood there and smiled.

141

The Great Gathering of Gods Soul

"To you, traveling stranger and sage," another family member called out and as it was said all in the room made a toast to him.

Satya and Barissa were quickly brought a glass of wine and they all drank to the toast.

It was a merry engagement, and the night was filled with such celebration and feasting that Satya felt heart warmed. Throughout the night, Vittoria's family members came to him in merriment telling him the story of the length of time that they all had been apart and why. They spoke about the land that had been in their family for centuries and the effect it had on their family when Vittoria destroyed it. They were sad at the way Vittoria succumbed to greed and for that reason destroyed what was in their family for so long. They spoke of how they all protested but she would not listen. Yet, although they were sad while recounting the events that led up to the party they were at, they all showed much excitement for her return to the Vittoria they once knew, the Vittoria before she was granted the deed to the land.

Satya inquired what she was like before and to all whom he inquired; the answer was the same. They said she was warm and thoughtful of others and cared about family. She was proud to be a Barbaccia. They said that after her divorce from Barissa's father she had become bitter and lost all her faith, not only in the concept of family, but also in nearly everything else that mattered to her. To his surprise a relative explained that Vittoria loved to read and had read every book on the shelves in the house. But now she did not touch books for the purpose of love or thirst for knowledge. The family as a whole had expressed to him how this night they had seen the return of their dear Vittoria's spirit and they were all filled with glee at the sight of it.

Then the food began to enter the room. He had never seen a display of food like it in all his travels. There were many Italian dishes, regional and non-regional, that filled the enormous table where the entire family sat. It was one of the most illustrious tables he had ever seen. The feast was placed so elaborately and

The Great Gathering of Gods Soul

delicately on the table, that it would honor even God, with its attention to detail and the magnificence it displayed. The aroma filled the room and consisted of a multiplicity of smells. The Antipasti of salami, olives, the bitter sweet smell of frittatas with spinach and ham, the smoky charred smell of roasted bell peppers, squid salad, Mozzarella toasts and salad leaves with gorgonzola. The aroma of roasted vegetables mixed with hot meat and the smell of so many herbs he could not distinguish lingered through the room. Then onion and tomato soup was brought to the table as the finishing of the antipasti, initiating the first course of the meal.

Pasta of every sort he could imagine was brought to the table. The servants were busy clearing away the plates as they were finished, making room for more. There was orecchiette with broccoli, spaghetti noodles with Bolognese meat sauce and mussels. Spinach and ricotta cheese gnocchi, risotto with shrimp, broiled polenta with gorgonzola, pasta with fresh sardine sauce and pine nuts and raisins, which smelled like the perfect mixture of salty and sweet.

The meat selection was vast and equally breathtaking. There was stuffed turkey breast with lemon, chicken breasts cooked in butter, quail with grapes, cod with parsley and garlic and roast pheasant with juniper berries. The smells of chicken and roasted vegetables, with the aroma of garlic, the sourness of lemon, the earthy smell of basil and sweet smell of hot butter were floating in the air and could only be described as the best dining moment in a person's life. The vegetables consisted of stuffed artichokes, asparagus and eggs, caponato with sweet and sour eggplant. The aroma of the pesto and fresh hot bread was delectable.

The crowds of her family ate and celebrated the night through talking to and loving one another. They were arm and arm with smiles upon their faces. Satya stood back and took one stolen moment away from the crowd to admire such togetherness and caught a glimpse of Vittoria affectionately hugging her daughter and kissing her face.

The Great Gathering of Gods Soul

Barissa rejoiced and he saw the look of healing on her face. He thought to himself how love could be recovered so quickly if given the chance.

The servants continued to rush in to expedite the removal of the almost entirely empty platters that lay on the table. Once the table was cleared, coffee and dessert began to unfurl. The Sienese strong bread, pan forte, baked apples with red wine, a decadent chocolate roll, chestnut pudding, tiramisu, custard ice cream and stuffed peaches with amaretto.

For those who did not want coffee, there was an assortment of aperitifs in heavy supply. There was Amaro Montenegro, Gynar, Fernet-Branca, Punt e Mes, Extra dry Martinis, Campari soda for the children, and for those coffee lovers who wanted a little kick, there was coffee Coretto. And last but not least, there was Espresso coffee laced with grappa or Italian Brandy.

As the elation of the party began to simmer, they all were sitting at the table and Vittoria stood up to say a few words. Looking at Satya, who was across the table from her, she began to speak.

"I would like to thank my guest Satya for helping me today. Because of our long conversation in the garden today, a place I have not walked out into for years, I have realized something," she said. "I realized that I have lost what matters most while on my quest for success. I lost not only my need for my family but even sadder, I lost myself. Business is not what is the most important," she said. "I forgot to cherish what was ancient and loyal--my family and this land. I hope that you all can forgive me?" she asked as her voice cracked and her eyes welled up with tears.

He smiled, knowing that he had helped her soul and that she would now have a chance to return to her old self. Her family swarmed around her with love, hugs, forgiveness and acceptance. As he watched the rekindling of her family his heart was filled with contentment, and he finished his coffee and zucotto. He received many smiles of gratitude from her family, and he could hear their silent thanksgiving and the words of their hearts speaking to him. Then in a wave of exhaustion he became very tired and knew it was time to leave to find a place to shelter for the night. As he stood up and said thank you for the evening's hospitality, Vittoria insisted that he stay for the evening. Gracefully he accepted and said farewell to the crowd, and the servants escorted him back to the room he had taken his nap in earlier. He felt happy for the joyous festivities and the rewarding evening. He knew that Vittoria still had work ahead of her to overcome her ways. Yet, in the presence of love, all things were possible.

Chapter Eleven

Birds of the Moment

He woke up the next morning and was invited for breakfast. During the meal, wonderful conversation ensued, which passed the day away. Each day that Satya was at the villa, Vittoria would invite him to a dinner meal at the days end, and ask him to stay another day, providing him with lodging. One morning at the villa turned into many mornings, until he had been there almost a month's time. Vittoria required much of his time, as she had many questions to ask him if she were to make a philosophical change in her life. She continued to challenge his ideas, but each day, showed progress in understanding why changes were necessary if she were going to have a happy and healthy life. He stressed to her on a daily basis, the importance of balance in any lifestyle.

Then one morning he woke as the sun was coming up. Two little birds looked in his window while they struggled to perch on the tiny ledge of the window. One bird had a piece of straw in his mouth, no doubt to build a nest. As Satya rose to see them closer they stayed on the ledge and the brightness of their eyes looked at him as if they knew him. When they flew away he thought of Asha and Ke'ren and knew that it was they who visited him through the birds for that moment, letting him know that they had been with him during his experience in that house, guiding him, just as he had requested. With a feeling of happiness and love he freshened up and decided to walk around the house while all were still asleep and find a special spot to meditate. He walked from his room and down a different set of stairs that he had not seen before. The stairs led to another room of brown and gold marble floors, subtle yellow lighting, and mirrors adorning the walls. He felt a warm ambiance in the room and decided to sit on the marble floor, enjoying the morning darkness and began his morning meditation.

146

As he sat in the middle of the floor in the large open walkway, he closed his eyes and went into a state of peaceful nothingness. Where he went was a revered holy place, which only the dedicated and wise could achieve because of the stillness of their mind. It was black and quiet in his mind, and he had learned to cherish those moments. Each moment would take him where he was meant to go, and he had faith in its peacefulness and also in his visions when they were given.

As he sat there, lost to the world, a face appeared to him in the darkness of his meditation. The face was old, ancient even, and he was surprised to see it as he was not expecting a visitor. With no words needed, he telepathically asked the visitor who he was.

"I have owned this land for generations," he said. The eyes of this ancient one were dark, like black olives, and his face was lined with the deep folds of wisdom and a life of hard work. They were wrinkles that could only be earned from a life of difficulty and hard labor. No doubt the conditions he experienced working in the fields that Vittoria demolished.

"Why do you come to me?" Satya asked him.

"We have tried to sway her, but she would not listen," the face said.

"And all the problems in her home and businesses; the flood of water to this land?" Satya asked.

Then immediately he heard the sound of laughter, echoing laughter of not one, but of a host of people together. He knew then that the spirit had not come alone and that it was the family of times that had passed; who had slaved over that land and now could not rest. They were disgruntled spirits from the destruction she caused, and they had been the ones responsible for all the unrest in the house and in her businesses. The ancient spirit explained to him that they had even tried to flood the land to get her to stop. But even as she had spoken to Satya in the garden, *nothing was going to stop her.*

"What is it that you want?" Satya asked the old spirit.

The Great Gathering of Gods Soul

"Retribution," he said firmly and angrily. "We will not stop until we get it," he said and faded out of Satya's inner world of meditation.

Shortly after the ancient one was gone; Satya slowly came back to his consciousness of the physical world and when he opened his eyes he felt a sense of urgency. He knew that he must speak to Vittoria at once. To his surprise, she was sitting on the floor in front of him staring as if to inquire about what he was doing.

"I must speak to you at once on a matter," he said to her with haste.

"All right," she replied with openness to his request. "Speak to me."

"I was visited by your ancestors in meditation just now. It is they who have been in this house, interfering with things, whispering to Barissa, all in an attempt to get you to pay attention."

"Pay attention to what?" she said somewhat defensively.

"To family and how the decisions you make affect everyone. They want you to understand the pride and love that went into the land. They want retribution, Vittoria, and they will not rest or stop your downward spiral until they get it."

With a quick look of disbelief, she gazed at him and then submitted to their request.

"How do I rectify this? I cannot turn back time, so I am not sure how to do as they ask," she asked him sincerely.

"Well," he said as he thought to himself. "You cannot undo what has been done. But you can continue to put your family first and include them in any future changes that takes place with the land," he said contemplating. Then something came to him. It was a way that she could rectify what she had done.

"What land do have you left?" he asked her, and he saw her eyes light up at the thought.

"I did not build on all the land, although I did plow over all that was left of the garden and vineyard," she said.

The Great Gathering of Gods Soul

"You will have to restore it back to its original state and give back, not only to your family, but to the people of this region, what you took away from them when you destroyed it all. In doing so you will restore the balance in your own life and family, but also in the agriculture here in Siena. I believe *that* will satisfy them and then you will be set free."

"I can do this, Satya. Money is no object to me. I will start organizing it today and have workers in the field by tomorrow," she said in her business voice.

He could see by the look on her face that she was already in her head mapping out the plans, so he began to excuse himself. "I must go now," he said with a smile as he tapped her knee. "You have much to do." When he stood up she asked him to stay in the villa.

"My dear Vittoria, my stay here is complete. In the blink of an eye your life can change. It is just that easy when we allow it to happen. Besides, there are others to interact with. I feel their pull and so I must go," he said. With a smile and a nod, she walked quietly with him to the door.

"Please tell Barissa goodbye for me," he said, bowing his head in honor and respect for her and the changes she was making. Leaving the villa, he did not look back. He had learned that it was only important for him to teach, and what others did with their awakening was up to them.

About a week later he found himself in the markets as had become his custom in the early morning hour. He admired the life and love that went into all that was sold there.

When he passed a little market and deli, he saw the head of a boar hanging above the entrance. He could smell the garlic and assorted spicy meat sausages that adorned the arched opening and cartons of packaged alcohol laid in the front with a hand written paper telling the consumer the price. Ivy ran up and around the arch entrance of the deli adding to its charm.

He continued to walk and view the open fruit and vegetable stands of apples, oranges, lemons, lettuce, celery, zucchini, potatoes, carrots, olives and a basket of sun-dried tomatoes, in vibrant colors. There was an earthy smell, a mixture of dirt and grassiness in the market because the vegetables were freshly plucked from the fields. The apples smelled sweet and tart, the way they smelled at perfect ripeness. Plastic bags hanging everywhere along the walls and cardboard signs were sticking out of the fruit and vegetable bins with daily specials and prices, written in red ink. There was love in the markets and he felt immersed in it. It brought back the memory of how he felt in the rice fields. He watched the people in the market who loved and cultivated the fruits and vegetables enough to help them grow. He understood what went into the stage that brought them to that market and so he felt a special connection to the market as it brought back happy memories and was an opportunity to reminisce about those who have touched his life in so many ways.

It was a lazy, sunny day, sufficient only for strolling when he heard the shout of his name. He turned toward the sound and saw Barissa running his way. When she reached him, he creased his brow with worry and held out his hand for her to hold.

"What is it?" he said with concern.

"Mother told me what you both had decided she should do to make things right. To make the voices go away and the problems stop," she said in a panic.

Satya was quiet and waited for her to continue.

"SHE SOLD THE LAND, SATYA," she cried out. "Developers came yesterday, and she sold it to them. We will never be able to make amends now," she said and looked down and began crying the saddest sob he had ever heard.

Satya's hopefulness for the woman turned to degradation and all the work and patience he had applied; all had been worthless. He wondered how she could see the light of promise and choose to walk away from it? How the answers to life could be given but if given to someone who was not asking the questions, the answers held no value. She was surely that person. It was not enough to learn the truth, but to live it every day by the choices a person makes in their daily life. He recalled the look of understanding he last saw in her eyes but in his

The Great Gathering of Gods Soul

absence she fell prey to greed once more and went back to her old ways.

In frustration, it made his life's work seem futile. He had begun to see that only some would actually practice what they had learned. The majority would be Vittoria's, going back to what was comfortable, even when it was wrong, selfish or hurt others in the process. People were willing to sacrifice family and togetherness for the love of money. They were like dogs returning to their vomit.

His eyes and body language showed his despair for the events that Barissa had just confirmed. "I'm sorry, Barissa," he said softly as he held her hand and looked down.

"What can we do, Satya?" she asked him frantically.

Satya put his arm around her, focusing on her sorrow before his and began walking with her.

"There is nothing we can do. Perhaps now that we have done what we could, we must let it go and accept that this may be how it was written," he said and looked at her. Barissa looked at him and seemed disappointed with his answer.

"Remember, Barissa, someday this will all be yours. Perhaps you will be the chosen one to make things right again, in the future. Maybe that is why the spirits talk to you?" he said.

"But the voices, Satya. I will go insane if they continue," she said with fear.

"These are the voices of your ancestors. Listen to them and ask for their guidance. They will help you and instruct you in the path of goodness. They will help you restore what was lost," he said to her. "Do not be afraid."

Although her face still had the look of panic and disappointment, it softened slightly. "Okay, Satya," she replied. "I understand." Then she kissed his cheek and said goodbye in a whisper, smiling through her despair. As she walked away, he felt sad that he could not do more for her, but all that he could do had been done. He understood what it must feel like to be a parent and watch a child go through something they could not help them with. Some lessons must be dealt with alone to build character.

151

When she was gone, the feeling of anguish and frustration filled him again. He was pained by the reality of mankind's inability to change or want to do a greater good when they had the opportunity. He blamed the selfish tendencies of mankind for the current state of the world. With all the progress of the world, still not much had changed. The planet only seemed to get worse, even with all modern technology and medicine. Greed always came in to wipe out the good that could be done and so there was never any real progress.

He had felt smaller tremors of disappointment to his being before but never on this level. He felt that there must be a more profound lesson that would be revealed to him, to make this lesson valuable in order to better his work to help mankind. But the more he tried to help mankind it seemed to make no real difference. With this melancholy attitude, he walked to the old familiar park to visit his old friend *Tree* in the park. He wondered what it would say to him in the form of quiet solitude to help comfort his aching soul. As he walked and finally reached the park, he asked over and over in his mind, what he could do to salvage the world? He would sacrifice everything to save mankind from their destruction, if given the chance.

He found his friend *Tree* and sat near it all day quietly. He read a book that he had in his small bag until the sun went down, and he spent his time contemplating his purpose, the places he had been and all that he had done with his life so far. When the sun set he lay next to the tree where he planned to sleep for the night. As he looked up to the sky his mind began to play with lighter thoughts. He began to play with the ideas in his mind as he had learned to do when he was on long journeys by himself with no one to talk to. He looked at the moon that was full and shining brightly and wondered if it was an observation planet. He wondered if those who wished to live on earth could watch mankind from the moon first, just to be certain. He had always felt watched on a full moon and laughed to himself at the idea. He pondered the humor of his thought because as strange as it sounded, it felt true to him.

The Great Gathering of Gods Soul

He then thought of the sun and all its glory. He wondered if it was merely all the great spirits behind the sun pulling all their energy together to generate life-giving light to earth. He wondered if the sun was a place where high-toned beings were busy with bringing the light of knowingness together to shine it on earth to sustain life and create awareness.

He stared at the moon and pondered his thoughts. He heard the sounds from the nearby streets and shops that seemed louder than usual. It sounded like loud voices and hammering, so he looked over to see by streetlight and the glowing solar street signs, that random merchants were boarding up their store windows. Although it seemed strange to him, he was tired and decided that he would investigate the oddity the next morning.

He closed his eyes and took in the refreshing night air breathing deeply and beginning to feel at ease again. But when he looked up, twelve strange men were surrounding him. The light of the moon was dim, and he could barely make them out. He struggled to see them in the shadowy night but all he could glimpse was their identical black suits and expressionless faces impossible to read. He quickly raised his back off the ground to protect himself from this mysterious invasion, but they were too quick.

"We're sorry Sir. As you requested," they said as they threw a heavy cloak over him. As he struggled to get up, he smelled a fume that shocked his nostrils. As he drew in a gasping breath he became discombobulated, and the dark unconsciousness came over him.

Chapter Twelve

Evocation

He woke up groggy and with the feeling of floating. As he came back to his consciousness, he jumped to his unsteady feet. Quickly acclimating himself, he realized that he was on a plane aboard what seemed to be a small private jet. As his eyes became clearer, he saw the twelve men that had abducted him. They were motionless, expressionless, statuesque and mysterious. He had no idea who these men were.

"WHERE AM I?" he demanded.

With little reaction, one of the twelve men spoke. "You are on a jet."

"I know that. Why have you taken me?"

"You know why," the man responded.

With confusion, Satya continued, "NO, I don't. WHAT'S GOING ON?" he shouted. "Why have you taken me against my will?"

At that moment, there was the sound of soft, playful laughter from the men. It was not as though they were laughing at him but laughing at the lack of his knowledge. It was as though they were aware of something to which he was not privy. Satya was confused and frightened.

"It is your will, Satya," the man said softly. "We requested a more gently way, but it was your wish to save time."

"What! Who are you?" Satya asked, still confused.

"We are your divine council." With a hand gesture pointing to them all, the man said, "We are the council to the Crown." The men looked at him as though he were royalty they were to protect. He soon understood that he did not need to fear for his life. He only wanted to know why he was taken.

"What do you mean, my will? I don't know what's going on."

The Great Gathering of Gods Soul

The same one of twelve answered his concern gently, "It will come, Satya. You will remember in time. Now please rest. We will land soon, and you will not rest once we do."

At that moment, calm came over him the way it does when a person lets go of control and begins to have faith. He felt that something was unraveling. He realized that these men were not hostile. They were aware of something that he would soon understand. His alarm quickly turned to curiosity.

"You are a great spirit, Satya," the man said.

With that, Satya sat down on the plush seat by the window, feeling honored at the comment and confused. He stared out into the distant horizon. He could see nothing but black smoke. An eerie feeling came over him, and he knew that what he was approaching was mayhem, an unraveling of events that was becoming clearer by the moment. He was always somewhere specific for a reason. At least it had always been in the past, and he knew this would be no different.

As he pondered the smoke he saw, he found himself feeling exhausted from the excitement and decided to do what one of twelve asked him to do, rest. Luxury was something that was far removed from the life that he had always known. He had worked hard to be nothing, as he wanted to call no glory to himself. He was not in service to mankind for reward or recognition. Yet in the lap of luxury, he found slumber and so it was that he fell into a deep sleep.

A long period of time had passed when he woke to the jolting motion of landing gear touching ground. He looked out the window to see a shocking sight. There were people running everywhere in a panic and clearing the way for their landing. He recognized where he was, Time Square, New York, and far away from the place that he had just been. He earnestly tried to get a clear view of what was beyond the black smoke that passed by the jet as it was coming to a stop. They landed in the street of the city, which was very unusual, and from the window he could see the sign that read, *Seventh Street*.

"What has happened here?" Satya asked the men still sitting in their upright positions and expressionless.

The Great Gathering of Gods Soul

"What has not happened here?" the one of twelve replied. "This is where it began, and it will spread everywhere in a matter of hours."

Satya asked again, "What happened here?" The one of twelve did not reply. Satya knew that he would get the answer soon, so he inquired no further.

The jet came to a complete stop, and the men all rose from their seats. Statuesque, they stood looking directly at Satya as if they were waiting for him. Although Satya did not know what was happening, he began to sense the words of the men they did not speak aloud and knew that they were waiting for him to take the lead to the door. Respect emanated from the men as if they gave him honor of a knowingness he did not possess. He felt he knew nothing but took the position he had always taken, which was to do what he must to help mankind. He stood and moved toward the door nervously, and the men followed behind him. When he reached the exit door, one of the twelve stepped to the front and placed his hand on the latch.

"Please step back, Satya," the man requested.

The latch was cocked, and the airtight seal was broken. Satya braced himself for what he was about to see. The suffering of man had broken his heart so many times and still he had never gotten used to the sight. The heavy door swung open and instantly heated and black smoke stung his face. He drew back in response to the shock of the atmosphere. He gasped for air and began to fall back. Quickly, the men assembled tightly to catch him and help him back to his feet.

Tears came to his eyes and there was tightness in his throat, as if he could not breath. He paused to realize what he was seeing outside the doors of the jet.

"Destruction," Satya said in a daze of disbelief. Trying to hold back the tears, they began to stream from the sides of his eyes and down his face.

"Yes, Satya. It is destruction on all fronts. Martial law went into enforcement a few hours ago. It is why we took you the way we did. There was no time to move slowly. World governments have issued a *global* religious ban. All holy establishments are being forced to board up their buildings and riots have begun in revolt to the theft of their freedom to choose their own beliefs," the man of the twelve said. "It began here, and it will be enforced world-wide by morning."

"Why have the governments done this? Why now?" Satya asked.

"The governments reported that they had reached their limit on holy wars. They believed to wipe out religion would limit the amount of war. But it is more than that, Satya, so much more. You asked why now? Now is the appointed time. The time documented in all holy books as the end," he said.

Satya looked at all the men in black coats as they nodded their confirmation to him.

"It is time," the other eleven said in synchronicity.

Satya could only stare at the men. He had heard of this day to come but never imagined he would see it. The end had been proclaimed for centuries.

"We must go," one of twelve said to him.

The jet had landed before an immense and awesome structure. The mere look of the building spoke of its power. Black walls and windows with mysterious looking silver etched borders surrounding each window. They appeared to be written messages in code.

They exited the jet and walked into the black smoke. There was the sound of firearms and the screams of the dying. He had never seen so much death up close and it was horrifying to him that he could smell the odor of burnt flesh. It was something that he would never forget or be able to get out of his mind. There were men, women and children in the streets in various stages of war and fighting. There were the sounds of gunshots rattling and ricocheting off buildings and even the cars in the streets. In the distance he could hear the sounds of what he thought were bullets hitting people and it sounded like lead pellets hitting heavy piles of dough. It made a mashing sound as it hit their flesh and he wanted to vomit when he realized that the sound he heard was indeed what he thought it was. The sound of gunfire, mixed with the sounds of screaming and the soot in his mouth from the billowing black, gassy smoke, made him gag. Groups were assembled and rioting, stores broken into and pillaged, buildings crushed to rubble, alarms going off and hateful words being yelled out in hostility everywhere. There was so much confusion that he was discombobulated. It was what his senses had told him beforehand in the jet. He had stepped into mayhem, and it was exactly what he expected mayhem to be. Chaos.

Six men had walked before him down the stairs and the rest behind him. When they hit the ground, their formation changed into a diamond with him in the center. He felt as though he had been in this place before, but he knew he hadn't. As they walked up closer to the building, the people on either side were yelling hateful things and rioting, but he was untouched by the seemingly invisible barrier that these men provided. He was encased in a diamond formation and protected.

As they made their entrance into the building, Satya looked up to read the immense and powerful sign that said, the *Vajra*. He had learned the word in his study of Buddhism. He knew the words well. Together, they meant thunderbolt and unbreakable. The twelve men split in formation once they had successfully entered into the long corridor into two lines of six. They were now standing in formation, six on either side of him, as they headed toward the elevator. They walked in perfect time with Satya, with him always in perfect center to their formation without missing a step. Their motion was spectacular and curious. There was only the sound of the echoing footsteps in the corridor. The doors to the elevator opened, and all the men entered so Satya followed. One of twelve pushed the button that read, *Highest High*, and they began their ascent.

The doors of the elevator opened, and he and the council piled out in formation. Again, they entered another corridor longer than the previous one. The walls were burgundy red, and they walked in formation toward the foreboding Double Black Doors ahead. He felt a different mood and tone from the corridor. It was powerful and mysterious. The men seemed to

The Great Gathering of Gods Soul

only have one goal—to take him to the Double Black Doors, and so they soon got to it and each of the men, one on either side, pushed the doors open and walked through them, maintaining the formation with Satya in the center. They were brilliant like poetry in motion. Satya felt the power of the room, and chills ran up his spine and arms. The room felt familiar and sacred to him as he looked around in awe. It was as if a myriad of men were meant to fill the room that was so vast. As he looked at the room, he felt as though the power of the room was a part of him, and his strength in body and mind began to grow. He asked no questions at that moment since he had recognized a pattern of the mysterious men to avoid giving an answer or if they did so, only in riddle. He knew the truth to be revealed with time.

He walked to the center of the huge room and walked toward the podium that was in the center of the room with seating like a coliseum. The room was cold the way rooms of that size typically were due to its immenseness. He walked down the steps to the podium floor that was sunken, and above and all around was audience seating. There were Victorian chairs, elaborately designed with woodcarving and red velvet cushions to match the burgundy red walls. Each arm had a small microphone attached to it allowing the speaker to hear comments of the audience. Everywhere he looked overhead was the sight of delicate crystal emblems. They were magnificent to the eyes as they were of every twist and shape. It appeared they could reflect any light whatsoever and were hanging from the ceilings. They reflected even the black light from outside and cast eerie black sparkles across the burgundy walls. There were thousands of them everywhere. Something was written in them, but he could not read them since they were so high. Someone had put love into each design and scrolled a message on them. But the messages seemed to be written in some ancient language, unreadable to the common eye. He was intrigued by the room and felt an ambiance of greatness in it. Still, he could not forget the shrieking and dying happening outside the massive room. He could see the black smoke outside the windows and was reminded of the terror and it brought back his nausea.

159

As he glanced out, he moved beyond the podium, but the men did not move with him this time. The view was breathtaking. All three sides of the room were full floor to ceiling windows with the view of what was once a beautiful city. Now, there was only black smoke and destruction, but inside it was silent, eerily silent. He approached the window and gazed out, noticing that for the first time since he had left the jet that the men had not followed him. He looked back at them, and they stood in formation at the podium as they had when they entered, six on either side. He pondered a thought while the men's eyes stayed fixed on him.

"I am to speak here, am I not?" he asked, looking at the men. The men did not move or speak. He did not need them to, he knew.

"I know now," he said out loud while staring into the world of destruction outside. "This is not Armageddon, is it?" he asked the men rhetorically. "This is the end of Armageddon. The end of the hell that mankind has made for themselves." He stared into the destruction. "I do remember now."

After a brief silence, the one of twelve spoke, "The great gathering of the gods has come, Satya. All those who have been worshipped, honored and feared, will gather here tomorrow to settle this matter."

"They will come in body form?" Satya asked.

"Yes, Satya, they will. There is no other way. You will recognize some who had taken fleshly bodies on earth to walk with mankind to help them. The others are very mysterious, some never seen before, only heard of and worshipped through faith."

"What matter is it that we will settle?" Satya asked. "There are so many."

"Yes, but all narrow down to just one, as you said to the men in the café," the one of twelve replied.

"How did you know that?" Satya asked, quite surprised.

"It is written, Satya."

"Will we settle who the true God is and whom he represents?" Satya asked.

The Great Gathering of Gods Soul

"No, Satya, you will settle the matter and you will have seven days to do it in. The same as the Creation."

At that, Satya turned his face back to the window with deep thought. He felt no worry but instead felt peace come over him. It was what he had worked all his life to do, to help all whom he could reach. It was the answer to the prayer he had made in Siena, in his frustration. He asked the universe to let him help save humanity and sacrifice everything for them and he was granted his wish. He was challenged and inspired. He felt as if his entire existence had been training for this very moment and the ones that would follow.

"Why me?" he said softly.

"Because you are nothing Satya. By being nothing, you are everything. You are chosen and you have felt your calling all your life. Your life has all been for this. All your struggles and hardships have not been in vain," one of twelve answered.

"Please, show me to my room for sleep. Tomorrow is the day?" Satya asked.

"Yes," one of twelve replied.

Satya sighed deeply for finally being acknowledged after so long. There was a moment of silence as there was nothing more to say. They exited out of the Highest High, through the corridor, down the elevator and to his room. Satya went into the luxurious room and the men shut the door behind him. He was alone and began to plan his first day with the gods. He spent hours compiling a list of all the wrongs of the world. While preparing, he began to worry and then stopped. He agreed to himself that he would not plan excessively, for he had lived the woes of the world and could express them well. He broke down all the errors of the world into seven sections and thus formed the foundation and outline for his talks each day. His thoughts were clear on each point and now he was armed with an outline and a platform to deliver his message to the most important crowd he could ever wish to speak before: The gods of all nations.

Later, he went back to the door and opened it slightly to see that the men had formed a half hexagon to barricade his door. They did not sleep, nor did they move the entire night. Dusk became dawn, and Satya was startled awake by a loud knocking on the door. One of the twelve entered before his bed with a message.

"Three hours before the great gathering, Satya."

Then he turned and walked out of the room in the same statuesque manner that he entered and returned to his formation outside the door. The door slammed shut.

Satya rubbed his eyes, remembered at once what the day would entail and felt a slight turn of his stomach.

"Let the games begin," he uttered under his breath.

As he groomed himself, he felt the sacredness of the day, and knew he would petition for the souls of man and how they had developed over the years. He would tell the gods of the good they had done and tried to do.

He watched the black glow of what used to be the sun coming up and felt at peace. He was not overwhelmed with the challenge at hand. Perhaps, it had something to do with that feeling he had carried with him all his life. He had been lonely in his life many times, but never had he felt alone. He had always felt a higher purpose was guiding his steps and protecting his way. When he needed protecting he had been protected, when he felt anxiety, his soul was quieted and if he became haughty, he was humbled.

The prayers had gone out all over the world and all the people of the world had petitioned their gods, philosophers and shamans for help. It was the "appointed time." This week would be all mankind had to prove that they were worthy of survival. It was his aim to help the gods see that unity could only come if they themselves could achieve understanding, not just of the world's problems, but to reach understanding of each other. He wondered if a god could learn. Could a god learn to change?

As he thought these very thoughts, the gods, honored ones, even the demons, were entering the sanctuary. Things would never be the same after this day and week that would follow. It would challenge every rule in the game of life. Many of the gods had never set eyes on the other. What would transpire

162

The Great Gathering of Gods Soul

while they were together could be either inspiring or detrimental to the future of mankind.

The Vajra building had been the chosen venue for the gathering because of its historical inspiration. Many wonderful things had happened at the Vajra, and Satya knew its symbolic meaning. He put on his white linen clothes and opened the door to his room. The council received him and escorted him to the elevator. They ascended to the top floor, the Highest High to the luxury view of the Vajra building. He thought back and remembered the news when the first Black American president was announced from the Vajra building. It wasn't long after that when the first woman president was elected as well. Impoverished countries filled with starvation were freed from scarcity and taught to help themselves from this building. But unfortunately, the teachings failed later because they were not applied with compassion for all. People who sat in the very room to which he was headed and strategically planned a way to help the world's people had brought down dictators. For those reasons and so many more it could have been said, *this is why the Vajra was chosen.* But that would have been vanity and also incorrect. It had been chosen for one reason only, for what the Vajra meant and stood for. The word *Vajra* had a double meaning. It meant *Thunderbolt* and *Diamond*. The word *Vajra* connoted immutability and something unbreakable. As he anticipated that what would be discussed during the week would shake their foundations like thunder, the diamond beneath would be revealed, the answer would be immutable, and it would not break the gods. They would not be broken if their spirit of goodness were as strong as he believed it to be. Satya had faith, he believed, and he was ready.

The men walked him down the burgundy red corridor, six on either side of him, and when they got to the Double Black Doors they stopped. One of the twelve turned to him and handed him a scroll. He opened it and looked down to see what it contained. It read as follows:

163

The Great Gathering of Gods Soul

Divine Attendance Record
Book of Names

Xipe Totec, Agni, Durga, Ganesa, Ganga hanuman, Himalaya, Jesus, Mary Magdalene, Jehovah, Yahweh, Allah, Muhammad, Krishna, Buddha, Shakti, Shiva, Vishnu, Ezili Freda, Ezeli Danto, Papa Legba, Gede, Mahakala, Maitraya, Heruka, Hayagriva, Avatar, Brahma, Maya, Siva, Yama, Lakshmi, Sati, Aditi, Parvati, Kali, Manasa, Manu, Mitra, Nandi, Nataraja, Uma, Prajapati, Purusha, Radha, Rama, Ramachandra, Saraswati, Shashti, Trimurti, Soma, Quan-Yin, Ksitigarbha, Lingham, Lao-Tzu, Pa Hsien, Tsao, Shen, Ch' eng Huang, Men Shen, Confucius, Izanagi, Susanoo, Amaterasu, Susano-wo, Vzume, Kami, Kaze, Mikao Usui, Amenominakanushi-no-Kami, Takami-musubi, Kami-musubi, Omikami, Ashtoreth, Amen, Anthat, Bast, Satan, Hathor, Hu, Isis, Khnemu, Maat, Nut, Ptah, Sebek, Aker, Anubis, Heavenly Father, Baal, Bes, Azazel, The Grigori, The Nephilim, Barbatos, Beelzebuth, Moloch, Baphomet, Balam, Volac, Uval, Sallos, Belphegor, Pazuzu, Marchocias, Paimon, Dagon, Belial, Lucifuges, Horus, I-em-hetep, Khensu, Nephthys, Osiris, Martin Luther King , Ra, Sekhmet, Huaxtec, Tlazoheotl, Tonantzin, Gandhi, Teem, Teotihuacan, Xochicalco Huehueteotl, Totonac, Xiuhtechtli, Hubbard,Chaac, Cocijo, Teotihuacan, Chalchiuiticue, Kukulkan, Ehecatl, Quetzalcoatl, Mixtec, Horus, Apis, Heqt, Anubus, Thoth, Gilgamesh, Mary, Mater Matuta, Xorathustra, Zoraster, Bahaullah, Lamai, Dyfed, Apollo, Mercury, Lugus, Lugh, Rumi, Bellona, Mandela, Jihad, Danbala, Eyeda Wedo, Iblis, Imlu, Forseti, Atlas, Orion, Cacus, Zeus, Saturn, The Satyrs, Sibyl, Ra, The Titans, Venus, Typhon, Vesta, Vulcan, Xanthus, Balius, Aine, Amaethon, Abarta, Prometheus, Achillis, Actaeon, Autonoe, Lilith, Agamemnon, Atreus, Hephaistos, Alcestis, Alcmene, Ammilius, Ares, Hera, Aphrodite, Danae, Semele, Dionysus, Artemis, Athena, Atlas, Asclepius, Boreas, Calchas, Echidna, Cupid, Pengius, Demeter, Dionysus, Eos, Luck, Boann, Camuos, Llvr, Cliodhna, Cernunnos, Dagda, Dana, Dian Cecht, Taliesin, Aonghus, Don, Dylan, Mabon, Donn, Edona, Mac Cecht, Macha, Manannan Mac Lir, Nemglan, Lakshmi, Mother

Teresa, Nemain, Morrigan, Teutates, Taranis, Loki, Satya, Aegir, Aesir, Balder, Dazhbog, Freyja, Frigg, Gefion, Sif, Idun, Jumala, Kied Kie Jubmel, Lieb-Olmai, Luonnotar, Menulis, Mimir, Nerthus, Njord, Thenorns, Ottar, Patollo, Perkuno, Potrimpo, Rig, Saule, Svantovit, Freyr, Tapio, Triglav, Tyr, Vrd, Tuoni, Thevanir, Vidar, Wayland, Adad, Ea, Adonis, Aglibol, Ahura, Mazda, Al-Uzza, Al-Lat, Alalu, Anu, Amon, Anahita, Anat, Anbay, Ahriman, Anshar, Anubis, Apep, Bastet, Ptah, Khnum, Sebek, Marduk, Astarte, Aten, Attar, Attis, The ba and Ka, Thedjinn, Dumuzi, Inana, Asha, El, Enlil, Ereshkigal, The Fravashis, Gadd, Garbiel, The Hafaza, Hahhimas, Hannahanna, Haoma, Hathor, Hazzi, Heptat, Hubal, Hupasiyas, Apsu, Vohu, Wado, Wadjet, Yam, Aditi, Adibuddha, Airavata, Aksobhya, Amitabha, Amaghasidohi, Asparas, The Asuras, Avalokiteshvara, The Avatars, Bandara, The Bdud, Bhagiratha, The Btsan, The Daityas, Dadimunda, Upulvan, Devi, Gandharvas, Indra, Ganga, Hshen-Lha-Od-Dkar, The Guardian Kings, Heruka, Hevajra, Kaldevi, Khyung-Gai-Mgo-Can, Korrawi, Katargama Deviyo, Karttikeya, Kun-Tu-Bzan-Po, The Lha Dre, Mahakala, Maitreya "Friendly One," The maruts, Mitra, Prithivi, Prajapati, Rakshasas, Purusha, Mahadevi, Rishis, The Sa-Dag, Surya, Tara, Upulvan, Batara Guru, Basuki, Barong, The Bajang, Batara Kala, Benten (Benzai), Bishamon, Boru Deak Parudjar, The City God, Ebisu, The Earth God, Dainichi-Nyorai, Diya, Daikoku, Ec, Erlik, Emma-O, Esege Malan Tengri, Fu Xi, Nu Gua, Es, Fudo Myoo, Fukurokuju, Fugen-Bosatsu, Gong Gong, Gao Yao, Gimokodan, Guan Di, Guei, Hachiman, Hikohohodemi, Hinkon, Olorun, Yu'cahu, Atabey, Shekinah, Baba, Maula, Om, Rama, Hari, Gobind, Madho, Wah-I-Guru, Radha Soami, Amaterasu, Ida-Ten, Ila-Ilai, Langit, Inari, Irik, Itchita, Izanagi and Izanami, Dorje Palmo, Jata, Juronjin, Kadaklan, Kagutsuchi, TheKappa, Khori Tumed, Kishimo-Jin, Lao Jung, Lei Gong, The Lightning Goddess, Marishi-Ten, Men Shen, Moyang Melur, Moyangkapir, Nga, Nagas, Naztha, Mucilinda, The Nio, NuGua, Num, Okuninushi, Ot, Pangu, Otshirvani, Pamalak, Bagobo, Polong, Mot, The San Guan Dadi, The san Qing Daozu, The San Xing, Semara, Setesuyara, The

Shichi, Fukujin, Shennong, Susano-Wo, Suku-Na-Bikona, Shou Lao, Tal Sui, Tai-I T' ientsun, Taiyi, Benten, Tomam, Tsukkiyomi, Uke-mochi, Ulcan, Umai, The Wind God, Wen Chang, Vizi-Ember, Xi Wang-Mu, Rangda, Barong, Yi, Yu Huang, Yuqiang, Zhu ong, Anza, Manu…

He looked over the list of names and inhaled a deep cleansing breath. Power came into his vessel, and he knew that his life was made for this very moment. He looked at the men on either side of him and said, "Stand back, this I do on my own." They respectfully stood one step behind him as he opened the Double Black Doors to the Highest High, entered with complete confidence and walked in before the crowd. The men followed closely behind, expressionless.

Chapter Thirteen

Day One

The Cry of Mankind

Standing before the gods, he understood that he was no one to any of these great gods. He was no one and gladly so. He knew that he who had nothing could lose nothing, so he spent his life working diligently at being nothing, at being no one. But it was a task that did not come easy in a world that valued status and judged against those who had nothing and little education. He was a feather floating in the breeze, for love's sake, and to reach a higher spiritual ground. Perhaps today was the day he'd see his purpose in fruition, for his whole life had led him to this very moment.

He stood before such greatness and the reality of the moment settled in his bones. The site of the crystal emblems that adorned the ceiling, mixed with his nervousness, took his breath away. His heart pounded. It was amazing to him that in the minds of such greatness and divinity, there came no answer to the world's condition.

He began to speak about the great distress over the condition of the world and their people. Some of the gods were moved to tears as they spoke of the prayers and pleas that had gone up to them. Krishna, with a face that was so soft and powdery white that it was almost a shade of blue, was dressed in a gold wrap and shawl around his shoulders made of fine cloth, a crown that pointed to the heavens and shined so brightly it was almost blinding. He spoke compassionately for his people seeking insight from Satya in order to help his people. As he spoke there was the sound of the many beads around his neck brushing together.

Papa Legba spoke up for mankind. His skin was dark from the burning sun of Africa and Haiti that he had endured all his life as a saint in a slave's body. He was very old and wore the cloth of the poor, colored baby blue, and had a walking stick to help him stand.

"My people are lost, Satya," he said. "I hold the keys to Ginen, our home land, but they lose their way once they have been shown."

Papa Legba looked at him with eyes hoping for understanding as to why they do not learn. Then softly, another god named Amaterasu quietly spoke up from her microphone with her beautiful and delicate face and Asian dress of red and white satin cloth and hair as black and silky as night. She was apologetic for the time when out of fear, she hid in a cave and plunged mankind into darkness. Then her Brother, Susano-wo spoke in his stormy voice from somewhere in the crowd and he had little compassion for the world. Amaterasu's eyes dimmed as she cowered, and the light of her glory faded. Yet, she did not stop looking at Satya. She wanted to help. Others, less compassionate, spoke up and he began to feel the personality of those in the room. He felt that they too were in pain for their people while others couldn't care less. Satya listened and then spoke.

"We are here today because the people of the world are crying out," Satya said. "Their cries, they say, are in vain. As we speak here today, there is war, senseless war. And why? Nations are fighting in your name, in the name of God. In the name of a god who will not help them, some say. Those who are leading the nations are serving themselves for power and glory. There is no glory to god in war, is there?" he asked them rhetorically. He already knew the answer. "Gandhi, a chosen one of God, once spoke a peaceful truth that I have never forgotten."

As Satya quoted Gandhi's words, he saw the face of Gandhi in the crowd, so humbled, so sad. He was dressed in rags and frail, so willing to take a body form again to come and help man. There was so much in his eyes, the imprints of the soul. In his eyes one could see the peaceful means the world could have but does not. As Satya looked at him and nodded, Gandhi spoke his very own words as he had said them once before, as a living god on earth, of flesh and blood, who walked the earth for the sake of mankind.

"There are causes worth dying for. But there is no cause worth killing for."

The room was silent as that profound truth lingered in the room and in the minds of the gods. The saying was still as true and as potent today as the time he had said it, so long ago while on earth, and in the body. It was man's rag of skin and bone that destined him to turmoil, trapped in imperfection and bridling the spirit. His mortal coil was worn in pain, and if lucky, had brief moments of joy.

Present in the room were gods of peace, gods of wrath and destruction. Maat, with her eyes painted in black, her long black hair and red dress with one strap over her right shoulder, wearing a single ostrich feather, came in peace. She was Egyptian and had long kept watch over her people to insure justice and truth. She was regal and had a sense of power. Her people honored her with reverie because she stood for all that was good and holy. And the people of Manat, the god of pre-Islamic Arabia, called him the controller of destiny and humanity. They prayed to him for meaning to their suffering and to alter the path they were on if it were treacherous. There was even Lilith, the goddess who looked harmless enough, yet she was winged and had the feet of an owl and a strange cap upon her head. Talmudic legend had it that Lilith was created at the same time as Adam, the first man created by God. Yet Lilith refused to lie down beneath him because she believed she was his equal. She flew to a faraway desert where it was rumored that she consorted with demons and became a mother to numerous other demons at the rate of a hundred each day. She filled the earth with all that could wreak havoc upon it. God had sent three angels to bring her back from the desert, but she refused. It was said that since that time, she had wandered the earth looking for unprotected children who deserved to be punished because of the sins of their fathers. She has been the secret killer of children, killing them with a single smile. Knowledge of her became so secret that most of humanity had

The Great Gathering of Gods Soul

forgotten of her existence. Yet, the mysterious deaths and disappearances of children have continued throughout time. It was evidence that her evil ways persisted.

Some gods had disciplined their people by fire or lightning, others by peaceful means. Some required sacrifices of their own children to the fire or even by the knife. Others of more peaceful means only required acknowledgement offerings such as fruit or silent prayer of gratefulness and devotion. With such extreme measures, it became clear why the problems of the world existed. For how could mankind follow the way of love and union when the people had seen fury as a means of devotion and others had seen a loving hand of guidance? If the gods themselves could not agree, then the struggle of the people would continue.

"The war of dominance exists not just with the nations but with the gods themselves," Satya said, looking around the room. "If you yourselves could not settle on a clear-cut way to communicate to your people, then how could you expect them to lead others in peace? Are you gods not also serving your own egos if your hearts are not selfless? Do you god's love your people enough that you would be their servant?"

Iblis, an arrogant angel and devil shouted out in exclamation, "It is not a god's job to serve the people, they serve our holiness." His words proved that he had disciples of his own and had created his own apotheosis.

"It is *that* ignorance perhaps that is the problem." With that comment, there was the sound of defensive chatter coming from the gods. "Just as a president cannot rule if it were not for the support of his people, then is it not the same that your people must choose you to rule them? Do you not have a responsibility to also serve your people?"

Iblis put his hand to his chin as if in thought to a good point.

"I would like to share a story with you. Once, I found myself walking on a dirt road on my way, enjoying the sun, when I was suddenly joined by a soldier still in fatigues and quite exhausted, nervous and weary. As he slowly walked with me on my path in silence, I sensed that he could feel my ease and began speaking to me. He opened up his heart to me as so many have before under uncertain circumstances. He had exiled himself from war and escaped battle, no longer wanting to kill in the name of 'freedom.' His mind was frenzied as he explained that he had experienced something of mystical proportion, a perception that shook his foundation to change him forever."

Satya looked around the room, and he had the attention of the greatest minds there. He continued, "He had believed in the cause of war, but in the trenches realized that mortality was all of which he could think. He thought of his own death and what it would do to the ones he loved. He found that he no longer was fighting the war of the nation. He was fighting for his own life. The lines of war were blurred and the reasons even more abstract. He began to question why was he killing those who, in another situation, could have been his friends?

"One day, he found himself face to face with an enemy soldier and on contact pulled the trigger first. The enemy was dead and although he knew that the enemy would also have pulled the trigger to kill him, he felt the pain in his own heart thicken. He no longer cared about this war. He hated what it made him do. He thought that no amount of money or patriotism could be worth killing for.

"As protocol would have it, the soldier disarmed the dead man. He noticed a photo in his breast pocket. As the soldier recounted the story to me, he fell to his knees and sobbed uncontrollably. The man he had shot was an Asian man who had a family, a wife and small daughter. The soldier felt such sorrow for what he had done, although it was his duty to do it. *His army was told to fall back and did. Yet, he continued to see the Asian man's face in his mind, and it was killing him.*

"For days after the shooting, the man's face continued to live in his mind and then he began to see his spirit with him everywhere he went. He could not escape what he had done. Soon mysterious things began to happen to the soldier. Strong urges to taste hot green tea and foods made for an Asian palate. He had a craving for foods he had never tasted before and even things he did not know of before that moment. He saw young children in the village and a deep fondness and joy came over him. He had a feeling he had never experienced before for children. He had none of his own and yet he felt a love for them as if they were. He was moved to tears and could not explain it until he realized this: That the dead family man had somehow walked into his body and allowed him to experience the things of his life that he would miss, before he would go. The dead man wanted this soldier to see his life as a man, the life he took away in a matter of seconds.

"But what happened next was unexpected. He felt the man's forgiveness. He could no longer fight as a soldier in a war that taught him to kill enemy soldiers. They were people and that was an awareness that he could not change or take back the awareness. He realized that 'nationalism' was just another word for 'desensitization.' The reality for him was that they were no longer enemy killing machines but were people, people who had families and also wanted to be alive."

Satya looked into the gathering of gods for a long minute, circling the room to look at them all.

"How did we get here? To the point that we fight wars and give it reason to make it noble? Is there anything noble about war?"

The god El, sometimes called Bull-El because he was known for his strength and said to be the creator of the earth, replied. "War must happen sometime, Satya. Man is imperfect and has put war in place to govern himself. We gave them free will; we cannot take it back."

Angry that they considered war as a tool, Satya said, "This world is full of young soul leadership self-serving themselves. Knowing nothing and acting on it. Who can we blame other than those who are in charge? Doesn't action follow leadership by example?" He looked at them to take accountability. "You are all perfect. Can't you devise a way to govern the people in happiness? Show them another tool without changing free will?"

172

The Great Gathering of Gods Soul

He looked around to see the gods shaking their heads no. Infuriated, he said, "You are great and mighty gods that fill this room we call the Highest High. Are the gods themselves under the delusion of the mind and its perversion of power? Are we giving the people of the world peaceful guidance or are we forcing them to live like jackals tearing each other apart? Fathers and mothers must guide their children. Protect them," he demanded.

There was a long pause of silence from the gods with the looks on their faces of surprise by his candor, and others, perhaps contemplating another way?

Allah cried out from the crowd, "What can we do other than stop this world in its entirety?"

Satya stared into the mighty crowd uttering these words in a whisper-- a whisper that was heard like thunder. "Yes," he said softly. "That is the question! It is for you to answer, mighty gods, not me."

Satya saw the sun that was setting in the sky, as seen through the large windows of the room.

"It is time to go now," he said with a hint of discouragement. "Please, go safely in contemplation of the things that have been said here today."

His council, who had been standing behind him in a half hexagon, filtered into a diamond with him in the center and escorted him out the Double Black Doors, through the long burgundy red corridor, down the elevator and into his room. Tired, he walked into his room, where he saw a simple meal had been laid out for him to eat, as the door slammed shut behind him. The men, again in formation, kept his door all night.

The gods? They went home in contemplation.

Chapter Fourteen

Day Two

The History of Hate

He woke up startled by lightning, which hit the ground and made such a noise that it threw him from his bed in a panic. The rain was pounding the Vajra so hard that he could not help but wonder if it was a foreshadowing of the days to come. He was touched by the intent of such great spirits manifested in bodies, these gods. He was nothing and still they heard his voice with validation and no doubt, went to their abode in deep thought and quandary the day before. He knew no easy answer would appear without first contemplation from the heart. That he knew for certain.

He dressed and groomed just as the day before and then rode to the top floor of the Vajra with the divine council; he felt a deep and troubled feeling inside. Today, he would address something that cut him to the quick. He opened the doors and entered before the gods. Standing at the podium, he announced to the great crowd, "Today, we must speak on things so horrible it pains me to speak to them." As he said these words, he felt himself holding back the floodgates of his eyes so much that the tears exited once again from the sides of his eyes. He had always been empathic and felt the pain of the world, even for the earth, as it sobbed its own destruction.

The gods sat silently and with confusion as they saw his turmoil within the first few seconds of speaking. He realized at that moment that the gods were far removed from life in the world and in the body. Some of the gods wanted deeply to know what provoked his pain. He could see the concern of some of their faces, those who had been in a body before and knew what pain really was. Like Jesus, Buddha, Muhammad, Confuscius, Papa Legba and so many others in the room, who had walked

174

the earth as a Dai-Ko-Myo, Bodhisattva, saint or prophet purely for the salvation of mankind.

"Today, we will talk about hate: The hate that fills this earth and destroys us all."

He saw the eyes of the gods looking the way a deer sees the light of oncoming traffic and knows its demise. Perhaps their eyes were so because there were many in the room whose ways of leadership perpetuated anger and hatred.

"This is where the world shows its baby soul. Although the people educate and show themselves obedient to their elders for a time, they are bewildered easily. They resort to hostility at the mere confrontation of an opposing view. The people seem to be comfortable in their rut of unhappiness. Although I see their desire at the same time for joy in their lives, they fear change and hurl reproaches or come to blows at the slightest injustice. All you gods lead your people differently," he said looking around. "some through peaceful means, others through fear and violence. Can we blame our people for emulating your history of events? You know who you are!"

There were so many gods in the audience, and he imagined many more that were mere visual dots to him, who, like Jehovah, the one he could see, had crinkled his brow at his comments. They must be thinking, *who is he to scold them,* he thought to himself. But it had to be said.

"How can we expect peaceful people when even the gods resort to fear, violence and dominance? Did we not settle this question with the attack on Job in the Bible? Wasn't the great demon unleashed on him to test his faith and answer the age-old question: Will man serve God with no reward and out of love?" He looked around the room and there were no takers to his question. Their silent resistance was disconcerting.

"How many 'Jobs' must we have to resolve that question? When will we hold back the great demon from our people so that they may breath in peace and not sweat blood from strife? Jesus, do you remember?"

Jesus did remember and felt deeply for the people; it was evident in the softness of his face and eyes.

175

The Great Gathering of Gods Soul

"Surely Satya," Jesus said. "I remember my own pain when I was in a body living upon the earth and the torment I suffered." Then Jesus stood up from his chair and looked into the crowd of Gods to speak in Satya's behalf. "You cannot know the pain of mankind until you have been in the body of man to know the sickness and pain it feels. The pain they suffer from injustice, imperfection and life's cruelties. I spoke up for the salvation of mankind and I was thrashed, my skin ripped and torn from my body and then nails driven into my wrists and feet to hang until I was dead upon a stake. All because I loved mankind enough to speak up to the rulers, for the people and the injustices they faced. All because I declared the hypocrisies of man; yet not all men are hypocrites," Jesus replied and then sat down in his seat.

Satya formed his alliance and many others whom he could see were peaceful gods and understood. There were the Devas who had divine powers to help human beings, and Vishnu who did all he could to protect mankind and establish the world as home for both gods and humanity. There was also Ganesha who worked to fortify mankind through wisdom and literature and was known for his assistance to man, in removing their obstacles. Ganesha seemed moved by Jesus, perhaps because he too understood the need to protect mankind from the darkness they lived in.

"In this world the people cry out from the horrendous things that have occurred. Have you all forgotten the acts of hatred on others because of the color of a man's skin? The starvation and gassing of men, women and children by a man who taught hatred to a nation and who almost annihilated an entire race? Who in this room will claim the man responsible for that? To which god does 'he' belong?" he said, staring them down.

There was no answer. "Surely no gods intended to create such a man. Or did they?" he asked.

"With great hatred, people have enslaved other people. Racism has imprisoned not only the victims but also the spirit of the ones who hate. They are covered by blackness and cannot

The Great Gathering of Gods Soul

breathe in the breath of life, life that is good and joyous. It does not come down to just one color against another; those of the same race have made a caste system to which those of a darker degree are the lesser people. Those of a lighter degree are greater. What does skin have to do with spirit? Spirit is not confined in a body. As Nelson Mandela said, 'We are free to be free.'

"Have we forgotten the great holocaust of women? Women were called witches because they dreamt to be more than they were allowed to be and forbidden by male dominance. They were women called witches and hung or burned at the stake for doing the things that 'you' gods gifted them to do. You made them 'free to be free.' The things that were innate for them to do they did. To heal and nurture and still, after all of this dominance and killing, their love for you prevailed? The people will not give up on you," he said, reaching out to their compassionate hearts. "Their faith in you is strong. They refuse to believe that you will abandon them."

The room was quiet as they listened, and although he knew that this was a courtroom seminar and he was the one required to do all the talking, he had thought there might be more interruptions or outbursts from the gods. *Why aren't they objecting or saying anything? Do they think so little of us that we are not worthy of a reaction even,* he thought. Still, he came to do a job, a job of a lifetime and perhaps his last? He has to speak the truth before the gods. There was no deeper honor than to be heard by the gods themselves, and so he continued, "There are some who speak of you with poison on their tongues and with manipulation. Like Bricriu the trickster. Do you remember him?" The gods looked at him with intrigue and some as if they did not care.

He knew they were aware of the old Celtic tale but nevertheless he went on to tell the story.

"His cunning behavior was sometimes helpful to the nation, but they could not control his behavior at all times. Bricriu tried to create a civil strife between three warriors, causing them to quarrel over who should receive the champion's

The Great Gathering of Gods Soul

portion of food at the royal banquet and who should have the privilege to sit at the king's right hand."

He continued, "Bricriu invited the court and threatened great calamities if they didn't come but the king ignored his threats. Finally, he swore that if they did not come, he would cause the breasts of their women to beat together until they were black and blue." With that there was a brief moment of laughter from the gods. "His threat worked," Satya said. "He then proceeded to provoke a quarrel that turned into an almighty brawl. His own home was in ruin and in the end the brown bull of Ulster and the white bull of Connacht failed to take notice of him when he stepped in to judge between them and was trampled to death by their horses. Or was it by his own trickery?" The gods pondered where he was going with his story.

"By allowing these calamities to take place in the world, are we provoking such cunning behavior that will ultimately cause our people to trample one another? Will we sit back to watch world leader after world leader break the spirits of millions, trick, deceive and lead them into destruction and death? Do not ALL people want to sit at your right hand? Are they not ALL worthy of such an honor? Will we reduce them all to fighting warriors led by another Bricriu? Will we use fear and mysticism to get them to submit or will we lead by example and let them know that they will all have a seat at your side and have a feast to remember?"

The gods began speaking to their neighbors, some in agreement with what he had said and others, less agreeable. Kali, whose name meant 'Dark One' spoke up in a rage,

"I lead my people as I see fit, mortal man," she said to Satya, leaning into the microphone and snarling at him. "They make their own choices. I do not force them to fight and kill," she said. Kali had been known for fighting demons but was often intoxicated with blood and threatened the world as well. The mere look of her was frightful as she wore a necklace made of skulls and had a third eye with red pupils painted on her skin between her brows. Still wearing the remnants of blood in the

The Great Gathering of Gods Soul

corners of her mouth and her skin, so black and smooth that it shimmered with tones of blue, she was fiery and seemed to have little control over her temper.

Satya stood at the podium and was quiet for a moment as he put his hands in prayer position to his lips and looked out into the crowd to see their faces. Such royal faces of wisdom and brilliance. He was feeling such frustration for having lived in the world he had just described and still they could not agree as a whole to help the people. He had hoped that those who had lived in the flesh on earth would understand and share their experience with those not in the position to understand such poverty, injustice and suffering. He could only hope they would understand as he held his hands to his lips as if in prayer and stared into the crowd. After a few moments of mumbling, it became quiet. Still, there was no answer. He had failed.

He went on: "Will hate to be altered so much that it will return to love once more? Please, gods, can you answer me that? Can you give us, your people, a shred of your justice and love that will overcome hate? Can you not only teach us to love but also how to love all? Can you remove the ignorance that drives hate and destruction of your people? Can you not only teach us to love one another but also more importantly, to love ourselves? Can you help us?" he ended with that question.

It had been a long day and he was tired from his badgering of questions hurled at the gods all day. The sky outside was dark and wet not only from the smoke and destruction but also from the setting of the sun. There were distant lights of an electrical shower, and he could not help but feel as though that same electrical shower had just run through his own body. He wondered if the way he felt was the way lightning felt after a storm. The way he was feeling at that very moment.

The divine council saw that he was feeling the exhaustion of the day and so with no further ado, assembled partially in front of his podium in a diamond formation and so he then turned around. He said no goodbyes to the gods. The men led him toward the Double Black Doors and once again, with him in

The Great Gathering of Gods Soul

the center of their diamond formation, led him out the doors, through the long burgundy red corridor, down the elevator to his room. He walked into his room and the door shut behind him, with the men outside again. A beautiful tray of food and drink had been set out for him to dine as though he were a king. He sat on the edge of his bed, tired from the day and feeling alone. He felt as though he was the only one on the planet fighting for human survival. Indeed, he was. He lay on the bed, and for hours he stared at the wall still feeling the effects of the horrible events that he had to recall throughout the day.

His room was warm and comfortable, the smell of meat and bread filled the air but as he looked out the window to his room, there was the black smoke of a destroyed world. He felt sadness and bewilderment, sickened by the past and fearful for man's future. He could not eat. He had no use for food.

As for the gods? He hoped that they would go home in contemplation, but he cried when he could not be certain.

Chapter Fifteen

Day Three

Pride and Leadership

Satya woke up early the next morning and felt drawn to the garden below. The garden had been built with an emergency dome with a hologram option normally used in bad weather. So, he went to the garden and as he sat in the garden of the Vajra, he thought of a quote by Rumi the Sufi poet. "The cloud weeps and then the garden sprouts." Rumi knew that man could not appreciate joy without pain. To know pain deepens the appreciation of joy when it comes. Underneath the lid of the garden there was no evidence of anything disturbed. The hologram played a beautiful spring day with no hint of the reality that really lurked outside. Inside the illusion there were no shrieks of pain, no screams of terror, no sight of the black smoke of destruction or the smell of burning flesh.

He could not help but think that in the last two days something deeper was growing. He was touched by the days that had passed. He found himself back in the place that had always made him feel at home. In the garden where the flow of nature was free, and there was peace in the scheme of things. He longed to help the world feel a shred of the peace that he had felt all his life, even amidst the storm. He had been a boat tossed by the waves all his life.

Yet he realized it was only through the currents of life that man can become a great captain of his own vessel. Without the storms in his life, there could have been no way for him to know his endurance and of what he was capable. Still, in the tussle he found himself as driven, as he had always been to uncover the pearl within the oyster. Everything he saw was beautiful, and when it seemed there was no beauty present, it was there just the same. Only covered by layers, as human beings love coverings.

181

Yet, it was the extremes of the world that broke man's spirit. The wars, murder, poverty and starvation could not lead a man to the water well of knowledge and understanding. He could not grow from the turbulence of life if he is dead, unprotected by the gods.

Once again, it was time to step into the elevator chamber that carried him to the room of greatness, the Highest High. Up he went to the top of the Vajra, where the world could be seen at a glance. The council piled in to the elevator with him and encased him the way a daisy closes at night to protect its day's eye. They walked down the corridor of burgundy red walls but then he was inspired to turn right and lost sight of the Double Black Doors. This time, he would enter the room through the side door. The council followed closely behind. He walked through the crowd of gods and observed them as he made his way slowly and calmly to the front of the room. They looked at him with confusion: Why he would enter from the servant's corridor? Walking down the aisle, he shouted out, "Is this not how religion can be? Entering from the side and diverting your attention from the real venue?" The gods looked around in confusion to his comment and change of entrance. Some of the gods whispered to each other about what he said.

Satya continued, "Through religious leadership, people are persecuted, judged and even killed in your name. How do you feel about that?" And as he said those words, his voice became choked up for a moment for he believed in good so much that it hurt. As he looked up, he saw tears in the eyes of many of the gods. Some felt the pain of being used to cause ill-will among men, in the name of what is sacred and holy. At last, he had found their nerve center.

The quiet voice of Quan Yin said, "It was not meant to be this way, Satya." Her eyes were glossy as she sat in the chair, her face was pale, and she had a ruby placed at her third eye. Her dress and necklace draped in many layers, and she wore her crown of compassion for the world. Her right foot was tucked under her dress with only her toes showing and her leg was up on the chair as she spoke. In the grand room, those gods who

182

cared were in pain of being used to create evil. It weighed heavily on their spirits to know that good was altered to negative.

"Living gods in the flesh have come to the people to guide them from this destruction," said El, a strong and mysterious Canaanite deity called Father of the gods and creator of the earth. "But they did not heed the warning. The body is limited to time and when the living gods left their bodies, the people resumed their destruction in my name, the name of God."

"Yes," Satya said. "They work tirelessly as over-achievers. These young souls love so strongly but in the blink of an eye will hate with equal zest. This is why so many times we have seen rallies of peace turn to violence. Does it seem to be the way of love? Love is altered so much that it turns to hate. Time distorts everything. We have seen proof of this over and over," Satya said.

"This system of things is so consumed with materialism, pride, ego and religion. The people seek out things to fill the void instead of taking time to realize that it is their spiritual need that causes this void to begin with. Each material purchase they make magnifies their void. Out of pride they cannot ask for help. Some would rather starve than ask their neighbor for a bowl of rice. What is worse is that some do this by having children who also go hungry because of their pride. Neighbors live for years next to one another and never reach out to introduce themselves."

Satya had witnessed how ego was very important in the ways of the world. That man's ego needs to be acknowledged even though it had been said that one should not blow his trumpet before men. For it is God who gives the glory, but man was not satisfied with that. Man wants titles that acknowledge their status, cars that show their net worth, endless sex because they cannot find the love in others when they cannot love themselves. The irony was baffling.

Satya continued, "Even in religion the leaders and go-getters want to control. The greedy and selfish do not allow those who come to worship only in love and devotion to do so. It

183

is not good enough. No, the religious leaders force the spiritual seekers to worship with their hard-earned money, their cold hard cash, or God will not approve of them, they say. The holy rollers control and pressure the people for money and pervert what is God into what is man in a morbid state. They force those with a holy calling to abstain from marital bliss when their own Bible warns against such a doctrine. Doesn't it say at 1 Timothy 4:1, 2 and 3 that in later times some would come, speaking lies in hypocrisies forbidding marriage and demanding abstinence from food and love. When it was that very thing that was given by God to be received with thanksgiving for seeking the truth? Then, being that abstaining from love is not natural, they turn on the innocent while wearing the cloth and bearing your name."

"The religious leaders tell the people that God loves a cheerful giver. Then they ask them to dig deep within their pockets for money they do not have to give and say to the people that if they give in faith, God will repay them. They know wholeheartedly that, although God does give in return, it is not always in the form of money that it takes to feed their children. The ways God gives are many."

The loving gods nodded their heads in agreement.

"Yet, the people are coerced and moved by guilt into it because they seek your approval. They want your love and so they are deceived. Should they feed their family on gratitude or thanksgiving? You did not intend that, did you? When the babies grow hungry, it is in God's name they hunger. And this has continued without avail. Then you wonder why our young grow up to hate you and not believe. Such atrocities go on in your name without recourse." He looked at the gods with confusion as to why they had allowed it.

"Yet, that is not the worst of it. Gods, dearest gods, are you aware of the biggest lie of them all? It is not enough that the supposed holy leaders put rules on how to love you but then they commit a far worse offense. People who claim to serve you diligently are condemning others with judgment for their level of understanding and ignore your words that say, 'Thou shall not judge.' I had heard of this myself in chapel after chapel with my own ears; Priests claiming divine knowledge of the scriptures and exclusivity by their own sect. Why, even I had studied the scriptures for many years and have learned that the truth is like a sunset. Each person can look to the sunset and report a different picture. Yet, it is the same sunset that falls. Even Solomon said that we could live everyday under the sun and still never know all that God has done. It is true. How could anyone of us who walk the earth have divine knowledge of all things?

"The great debate of your ways among men is this: Is there only one path or are there many roads leading to you? For this, the religious hate and condemn others in your name. So many people are persuaded that there is only one path to take. All those who do not conform to that way of thinking are told that they will burn in hellfire. Some religious people say that those who seek out the truth in other forms will spend an eternity of torturous burning that oddly enough was never mentioned in the creation, showing its construction and God's use for it. I have only heard of men talk about it in an attempt to control others with fear. I have looked for God's own personal description of this Hell in all of the holy books I could find. I had even studied the word Hell and found that it meant one thing in many languages. Hell, Hades or Sheol all meant the common grave of mankind. I saw no inferno anywhere. I only heard man speaking of it for his own intention. I have often been puzzled at people that have never questioned that fact. I have asked myself, *if God were to burn us for our sins, then would he not make it clear our punishment from the beginning*? Would you not list the place of our demise in the beginning of your holy books so that we are aware of this place beyond a shadow of a doubt? Gods of the heavens, have you heard these things that go on in the world?" he asked in sarcasm. "The people turn away from you because of the mockery man has made of your name."

"I understand," he said to the gods who cared. "Life has been made a game; this is true. In order to make it fun, you have set forth a puzzle for us to put back together in order to find meaning to our lives. But this is what concerns me in regard to your plan. These churches of man teach that if a person continues their search for you beyond what the dogma of the church has stipulated, they install the implant of fear and blasphemy. They say that this 'so-called Satan,' or various other evil spirits will carry them off the chosen path of the truth and he will lie to them. No doubt, the creators of this lie are in this very room. They teach that to search is to blaspheme."

The gods began to look around the room as if to see whom he was referring to. He could see noticeably that the gods Iblis, Dorje Palmo, Baal, his ferocious wife Anat, and Mot began to huddle closer together and snickered and made quiet comments to each other that Satya could not hear. Satan leaned back in his chair with a cherubic smile as though he was pleased with himself and had found glory in his plan. They were all, no doubt, fruit from the same tree of destruction and turmoil. They did not seem pleased to hear that Satya knew their plan.

"Yet how can they be sure that the churches are teaching accurate knowledge of you if they do not seek it out to narrow down the road that leads to you? How can man settle to one truth with no knowledge of what is out there? Yet so many do and thus fall into the traps of deception. It saddens me that they do not seek because when they do is when they see with a closer eye that we all are the same. We all love, laugh, suffer and ultimately die. We are all threads woven into the same cloth."

Some of the gods were noticeably touched by his humanity. He saw many that he could see clearly bring their hands to their lips in prayer or make some gesture with their hands that showed that their body language was warm towards him and his words. He saw the look in many of the gods eyes the way his own father would look at him when he was a child. He saw the same look of pride at a lesson learned or the look of a parent when a child takes his first steps or learns to do something on his own. It was a look of relief that there was understanding, and the gods seemed refreshed by his awareness and looked at one another with smiles while in their seats. Yet they were silent. Satya's body rushed with a feeling of warmth because he felt acknowledged by them.

186

"The more I have studied religion and philosophy to find you, the more that I realized that all cultures have similar stories of you, yet only call you by a different name. Through this knowledge, my heart has been filled with love for all people and it became less important to change a person's beliefs but to allow them to be who they are because they are all gods. They are all you. That is the game, isn't it not? Through the diversity, I have seen with clarity the union of the human race. I wonder about this world to help others as they need me and wonder how they cannot see such a peaceful and accurate truth. But I have realized that we are all on our own journey and at our own level of enlightenment. So, with that knowingness it has become all right. Eventually, we will all get to that point of knowingness on our journey home." He poured water into his glass that was sitting on the podium and took a drink.

"I was, at one point, forbidden by the secular religions to seek you out in the world and it was then that I parted ways with the churches. I believed in my soul that if I ended my search on blind faith, knowledge of you would cease to exist and I could not live a life that way. For in me you have put the innate desire for knowledge. While taking my pilgrimage, I began to contemplate this very thought in regard to religious teachings: What if the lie is the teaching itself that there is only one way instead of many ways to reach God? As they say, Satan teaches that there are many ways to God, and it is a lie. But then a thought came to me that was very profound. Are we to believe that this Satan, who is called a liar and betrayer, would tell us outright what his plan is? If he were to tell the lie of all lies, would he not lie about searching for God? Could this Satan or various other evildoers really be using the religious leaders to teach their lie which is to stop the search altogether? Wouldn't that be the victory of all victories for them?" he asked the gods.

There was a look of fear on some of the hateful gods' faces that was a clue that a truth had been revealed. It was clear that Satan was pleased, still reclining in his seat with a pleasant grin on his face while the others began to clamor. It was unclear who was saying what words, but he saw the face of Kali shouting at

187

him as well as the others. Their faces were frightful and the mere sight of them even in silence was scary. He heard the word *liar* being shouted at him and the sarcastic snickers saying that he did not know what he was talking about. Yet, with the rage they were doing he felt no fear. There was joy building in his heart because he knew he had been right. So, he ignored their viciousness and directed his attention to the gods who wanted peace.

"There are questions, dear gods. Will the religion of the world be changed so much that it will inevitably return to you? Will you continue to allow those who seek you out with a pure heart to be condemned and persecuted by those who use your name deviously? Lastly, the people ask this question most of all. Is there a greater purpose to all this suffering or will you allow the people to wander hopelessly and inevitably, godless, for time indefinite? Will this suffering go on forever? Until now, this appointed time—these have been the things that they have wondered about."

The evil gods looked at Satya as if he were foolish and had no comprehension of their works. The other loving gods remained silent to his question, and he felt frustrated that they did not live the hardships of ordinary men and could not understand his need to know their plan. The evil gods were arrogant and uncaring of the suffering of man. But the silence of the others puzzled him. Why would they not speak up to help him help mankind?

The council surrounded him once more and he said goodbye to the audience. In diamond formation they walked out of the Double Black Doors and down the long corridor with burgundy red walls. He walked in despair.

It was then that he noticed the unusualness of his council's formation. Although he thought it strange, he hadn't given it much thought up until now. He understood the spiritual realm on many levels and that spirituality was also mathematical and geometric. That the diamond he was encased in could also be two triangles on top of the other. His councilmen were methodical, and their little movements had significance.

Trying to flee the blackness of his soul in that moment he looked for something else to focus on and noticed the men and their shapes. He remembered the teachings from *The Philokalia* that triangles meant something very significant. They meant spiritual knowledge. That there were two, only added to its meaning. For two's in numerology meant idealism and healing. He pondered the significance of his findings as he rode the elevator to his floor.

As the council escorted him into his room, he then gave thought to the half hexagon the men would make outside his door every night. The hexagon was symbolic of the creation of the world. The *Philokalia* was written for the masters of the spiritual world and had taught him significance of shapes. Perhaps it was symbolic of the new world he was struggling to create with the gods. *Perhaps,* he thought.

Continuing his fast, he prepared for sleep and shut off the light. His mind raced with thoughts of what he would say tomorrow. His mind raced until exhaustion got the better of him and rendered him unconscious.

Chapter Sixteen

Day Four

Strong and Selfless Passion

The room was pitch black when he was awakened by a tremendous howl. As he came to his senses, he realized the howl was coming from below. It was the howl of a lone cat. In his concern for the animal, he got up and went to the window. He looked out the window to follow the direction of sound. It was coming from the garden courtyard. He could not sleep now that he had been awakened and so decided to see about the ruckus and if he could help the little creature in distress.

He opened the door of his room to find that the council was not guarding the door. For a split second his brow creased in confusion. He left his room and stepped into the elevator and was taken to the courtyard. The double doors opened, and he stepped out. It was so beautiful that he couldn't help but feel there was peace in the universe although he knew that to be false. It was 2:00 A.M: The hour he knew to be mystical as it was the hour that mystics say prayers are heard and life scrolls completed. It was the most documented time of death.

As he stepped into the heart of the garden, the tangy sweetness of lavender danced in his senses. He felt complete. In that same moment, he was recalled to the world by the howl of the cat that woke him. There it sat, white and graceful, on the garden pillars. It was a white Siamese with ocean blue eyes and red pupils looking at the full moon and howling once more. It took no notice of Satya at all as though he was not there and able to witness the secret life of the cat. It was joined by a second cat, which had come from behind — black with large ice-green eyes. Soon he heard a chorus of howling as they looked up to the moon.

He thought to himself in laughter, *they have forgotten who they are and are mistaking themselves for wolves, barking at the moon.* Without disturbance, he looked up also to witness the amazing fullness of the moon and how real it looked while he took a seat realizing that it was only a hologram of what once was a beautiful sight. The moon and stars had always been so clear during the hours the world was asleep. It was the stars' time to shine. Then he thought of a parallel thought. *How, just as these cats are howling like wolves, people are. They have forgotten who they are and do not see their own inner beauty. Human beings howl with the discomfort of their own tears of unhappiness and the loneliness of their alienation.*

As he sat and pondered over that thought, he heard a crackle on the other side of the flower garden where there were more benches. The cats also heard the noise and were startled away. He was silent for a moment so that he could follow the sound that was coming from behind him and began to walk to the other side to see who was there. He could feel there was another presence in the garden. When he reached the other side, to his surprise there she was, sitting on the bench gazing into the moon—a beautiful young woman with strong features. Some would only see her stunning beauty, but he saw contemplation and intelligence in her being. Quietly he sat on the bench next to her and then said hello.

"Good morning, my name is Satya. What is your name?" he whispered.

She glanced toward him for a moment and then looked peacefully back up toward the moon.

"I am Jeziah," she said, never looking at him. She had soft blonde hair and a mesmerizing voice that was deep, gentle, and seemed to flow like the ocean.

"Why are you here?" he asked.

She did not answer right away. Then she spoke, "I heard the howling and once here, fell into the trance of the moon. It caused a deep contemplation in me."

"What is it that you are contemplating? You seem troubled," he said, hoping to look into her eyes.

She finally looked at him and said, "You're right. I am a mother of three and raise my children alone."

"Where is the father, if you don't mind me asking?"

"My children lost their father to drugs. He is alive but abandoned us to pursue the needle, and I was left here alone to raise them. At night when they are asleep, I fear that I am doing them an injustice with his absence. I worry that I am not enough to fulfill all the things a mother and father must be for a child. I have the burden of being both to them. I work tirelessly to support them, and it does not feel like enough," she said, getting noticeably choked up and disappearing into her own world of thoughts. She continued, "They are five, eight and ten. I could not know a greater love than the love I have for my children. It is more difficult for me to earn a living for them with no formal education and limitations on the hours I can work. But I have learned that if I must do anything, I must believe I can do it and then do it alone. When you came up to me, I was looking at the stars and wondering what God is doing. Is he happy that I wonder how he is?" she said, looking at the moon and the stars. "Does he feel the pain and loneliness of having no one equaling him, as I have no one?"

She sighed. "Sometimes I cry myself to sleep at night because life has been so tragic and unfair to me. But then I look back," she said with a smile, "and know that there are good people in this world. If I had not gone through these trials in life, I would not be the woman I am today; the woman who knows such love for her children, who sees God in every creation and seeks the deeper purpose of life's experience. I do my best to not indulge in self-pity as it serves no higher purpose and I know that my spirit is strong enough to take it."

She stopped for a moment, and Satya could see that she was experiencing a powerful feeling. He could see her face begin to glow as though she knew something that others did not.

"People don't understand, Satya," she said and turned to him. "They feel sorry for me. But I am the fortunate one to be aware that oftentimes the jewels in life are hidden in misfortune. I take comfort in knowing that some day I will leave my body

The Great Gathering of Gods Soul

and join the other world. I will keep God loneliness and so I will no longer feel alone. Until then, we meet here, in this garden."

Satya felt her peace and could see her contentment.

"Although I am challenged every moment of the day with providing sustenance, caring for my children and training them in the virtues of goodness and love, I am grateful. I know the secret of life."

Intrigued and humbled by her words, he whispered, "What is the secret, Jeziah?"

"The secret is simple. I am a spirit, not a body. There are only two truths in this world. *I am, and I create.* Everything else is a lie."

As she finished her words, she rose to her feet and said, "Go safely, Satya."

Taken aback by her sudden finish, he asked her a quick question. "How did you get in here?" he asked respectfully. "The building was closed off when the trouble began. Where are your children?" he asked, very concerned for their safety.

"I work and live here," she said with a smile and a calm spirit. "As for my glorious children? They are with me always and safe from any harm." Satya smiled in relief and respectfully took his leave of her with a warm smile and walked toward the exit of the courtyard. Intrigued so much by her love, gratefulness and strength, he looked back to glance at her once more. Trees, flowers and bushes were all that remained. She was no longer there to be seen. She had slipped away into the dark night of her soul.

As he turned back around, he saw his council standing at the entrance of the garden. They were there standing in formation waiting for him. They escorted him back to the room where he spent many hours reviewing in his head over and over, the conversation he had with Jeziah, her love, contentment and peace.

He spent the afternoon of the fourth day with the gods reminiscing the experience he had with Jeziah in the garden, using her as an example of the good that is still prevalent in man. She was a woman who had such a heavy burden, more than most could handle, but found grace despite it all and refused to allow the world to break her spirit. Although petite, she held such a powerful force and did not seem to feel confined to the limitations of her body the way others did. She made no excuses for her life, nor did she surrender to misfortune. She was spiritual and he wondered if Jeziah was hope itself. He wondered if strong passion could be used for something other than serving ourselves. *Jeziah's mature soul surely did,* he thought to himself. The love for her children was impressive and the impact on them would be enormous. What beautiful people they would become because of her, if the gods gave her and many like her a chance.

Many of the gods heard his story and from the expression on their faces, they seemed to feel the same sense of inspiration he felt from her. He saw the faces of some he did not even know by name, smiling and nodding. They looked pleased to know that someone of faith still existed. The collectiveness of the gods came together and there was a luminous glow that seemed to shine in the room. Satya could feel the energy emanating and flowing onto him and he accepted it as a gift. He thought of Jeziah's loving kindness, and how she gave with no real concern for herself. All the while, she felt an underlying feeling of sorrow at being alone in the universe.

"Is our strong passion directed at everything in life but the people who need our love?" he said to the gods. "We invest our passion in fun and games, work and turmoil, but do we really live to serve and help others for the sole purpose of love?" He walked slowly around the room pondering the thought.

"She asked a question that I will honor her with by bringing it to you. She wondered if you, God of all gods, felt alone in your unequaled power. All the while her only thought for herself was to be there for you when she leaves her mortal vessel.

Is this what it means to be selfless?" he asked. "Does anyone really practice this measure of love?"

"She is rare, Satya," Umai, the mother goddess of the Turkic people said with her tresses that resembled the rays of the

194

Siberian sun, her skin bronze and her words of motherly concern. "Most people do not care, unfortunately," she added, looking down and seemingly sad at the revelation of her words.

The mood became contemplative amongst the gods. They were calm and thinking. Satya was escorted back to his room in the same fashion as all the other days. He did not know if the gods left seeing hope for mankind, but he did.

He wondered about Jeziah and what it was in her life that made her selfless that way. He wondered why so many others could only think of themselves and knew that it was for that very reason the world was in its destructive state. *If only they all could be like Jeziah,* he thought.

He hoped to have the chance to teach the world to be more like her. That night, he got little rest wondering where mankind had gone wrong and what could be done to save their souls. He wondered until the wee hours of the morning and then finally fell into slumber.

The Great Gathering of Gods Soul

Chapter Seventeen

Day Five

Blasphemy and the Ruby Uncovered

The divine council stood behind him in the elevator that took him to the Highest High and opened its doors to escort him out. Standing in the corridor of burgundy red walls, he saw the Double Black Doors giving entrance to the gods. He stood before the doors, took a deep breath before entering and suddenly was hit with a vision that froze him.

He saw Jeziah's feet with a draping white silk robe caressing her legs as she ran to the latrine to lift the lid upright. She knelt over it and became ill, dry heaving. In his vision he saw her on the white floor, and he saw her hold her face in her hands and sob. She was not ill with sickness. She was sick for the condition of the world. As quickly as his vision came, it left him and he entered before the crowd, pushing open the strong Double Black Doors leading him to the gods. No doubt, they had heard the news.

"It is with a heavy heart that I come to you today. The people have organized. Several world leaders were executed in the night and the United Nations building was leveled. They are rejecting this Martial Law. Innocent people were killed in the explosion. The killing and destruction will continue until this is resolved," Satya explained.

The only sound heard was the drop of his tear hitting the podium. The gods had a look of concern and some with a look of intrigue to his human reaction. Some looked as though they too wanted to cry for his pain. The Wind God, tall, strong and gentle, began to open his mouth to ask a question but was not quick enough.

"Why do you care, Satya?" said an unknown ugly and hateful member of the Grigori. His hair looked like snakes and his coloring was green and black like a shadow. "You have a place in heaven. Surely you know that?"

"It hurts me to see the people fighting this way. I have been a pilgrim all my life, never causing pain to anyone. I have denied my ego thus, never having anything to prove. My only wish has been that the entire world could live my peaceful life and see that war and fighting is not brought about by the spirit, but in the constant wantings of the flesh. Why is there such a high premium on reigning supreme? Having all the power? It seems people want to emulate you but only in equating power deprived of goodness or compassion. I am tired of it! Goodness is being bullied out, where those of us who are peaceful people cannot exist in society. We are being smothered by badness. Why do you allow this?" he demanded of the gods. "Will you sit back and do nothing while we destroy ourselves?" Their silence made the answer apparent; they were. The vile and hateful gods laughed in glee because they knew that the indifference of the kind and loving gods was because they had given man free will and could not interfere. It was a divine law that had been set in the tablets of the heavens from the beginning.

"This morning, as I began the day, I heard the news of destruction and killing and heard the threat of a dictator to its people. He said that when this war was over and they have submitted, he would seek out the wives of the People's Party and torture them until their eyes bleed." Satya watched the brows of the gods frown with the same level of disgust as he had experienced.

"Does it appear to you as it does to me; that there is no limit to the sickness of a mind of a person who can offer such a threat? Does everyone turn a blind eye to the problems of this world, including yourselves?" he asked with disgust. "Can you not hear the screams of your people begging for your help? They are starving and bleeding and you sit and watch? Is it not in one of your very own holy texts that says, 'How can you say to your brother to go eat, drink and be merry when you know full well that they have no food or drink?' Why will you do nothing?

The Great Gathering of Gods Soul

"The people try to solve the world's problems, but they are not capable of handling such a feat. Man is self-determined and loses his control of the barriers that exist. He tries but ultimately traps himself in believing that he can do it all on his own. When he realizes he can't, he becomes discouraged and stops altogether. Even huge amounts of food are gathered by food drives yet do not always make it to those who hunger. Political parties use starvation as a means to control their people. It is pure evil to sit and watch a nation wither to death and do nothing. Yet, what can we humans do? We try and are defeated. We see the children so malnourished that their bellies are swollen and even the flies can smell their walking death.

"Won't you stop all this? Help your people in unity. Can't you work together to help them?"

The gods looked at one another and snickered as if it were a preposterous idea.

"This is YOUR challenge you are faced with, gods," he said condescendingly. "You all have mysterious ways. You have created a game which the people have lost consciousness of, and so do not know it is a game they are playing, nor do they know the rules to the game in order to play to win. Maya created the game as the Hindu story goes yet stole their memory and gave them longing instead. The soul longs to go back to its whole with no idea how to do it or memory of why they long in the first place. How can we return to the whole when we do not know there is a whole to return to? Why have you trapped us in this dreadful game?"

"We do not owe you or the people an explanation, Satya. It is what it is," said the Beelzebuth, who had a face that resembled a fly, with two tattoos of skulls on each of his huge shoulders. Azazel and Moloch agreed with him, nodding yes, menacingly. Satya just stood and looked at them.

"Many philosophy books have been written to explain the condition of the world. Why I have retained my cognition of this game, I do not know. But I will tell you this much: good and bad fill this earth. Human beings, in their limited search, understand that there is a need for good and bad. Without the bad, we could

198

The Great Gathering of Gods Soul

not fully understand or appreciate the good. Some understand that without the challenge of badness always present, there would be no resolve to pursue awareness. We know that through the challenges of life we learn the most about ourselves. Learning is the only thing that gives us a sense of reason to survive the repetitive suffering. It gives our suffering purpose. For if we had no purposes to our suffering, why go on living? Why continue an ongoing turmoil with no point or end?" he asked sarcastically. He was tired of being gentle with them.

"WHY DO YOU STAY SILENT? WE ARE BEGGING FOR YOUR HELP."

He looked around and noticed that the devious gods were watching those that were good, while laughing and snickering under their breath. The righteous gods seemed appalled at the tone in Satya's voice by the look of their faces, but Satya didn't care. He wanted a reaction. He noticed that the gods who had walked the earth in the flesh were looking at the others who had not as if they were waiting to see why the other gods had done nothing to help mankind all this time.

"Your ways are so diverse in styles that it is no surprise that the people follow your lead, reaching the journey to the middle, with swords. How can you expect peace from the people when you yourselves are not unified with one another? I say here today that we are not different as people. People are raised to choose a side and are taught that to seek is to blaspheme your name. I was not implanted with that idea and see clearly that it is a lie! I have studied you, more than I can number and have found this. Although you all have different names and all your own ways, the stories are the same that you deliver to your people. All of you have stories of the flood, creation, good versus evil and that the soul is promised life even after death. Even Christians believe in life after death, although it is in the form of resurrection of the body. Either way, the truth remains. Every culture has their saints and devils. Every culture or spiritual person believes in a life beyond death." He noticed Brahma in front with a grin on his face, amazed that Satya had figured out a truth. Sitting next to him was Jehovah and they looked at each other supremely and then at Satya with a proud look.

"I have benefited from seeing you all in your glory, even in your hate, with clear sight and no bias on my part. All of you, each one, represent love or its direct opposite. But how can people love one another when they are fed the lie that to seek you in more than one place is blasphemy? For it is in the seeking that the ruby is uncovered. It is there beneath the soft ground of your truth. Why, just thinking to myself now, I can tell you that I have seen parallels in the stories and myths. Wasn't it Jesus and Zoraster who were conceived through miraculous births? Weren't they also healers who performed the same miraculous healings on the people?" he said, stepping down from the podium. "Weren't Moses and Krishna switched at birth for their protection?" he said running through the crowd to where they were. "Aren't Iblis and Satan both fallen angels who became devils?" He walked in front of them and pointed them out. "Aren't Lilith and Satan the same snake in the garden of the beginning of man?" he asked of them all looking into the great crowd.

"Kali," he said shouting out to her. "Do you not see the resemblance between you and Dorje Palmo?" He pointed out that they each looked identical with the exception of their race. The gods looked around at one another seeing their similarities with the others as Satya continued. "I beg of you, help your people see. Give them the map to this game before they destroy themselves and delete this game you so enjoy watching, or before you delete it yourself in disgust."

"I understand that there is good and bad, because all that is, becomes altered in time. If there were only good now, then in time, there would be only bad because things are always changing. There must be a continuing cycle of equality between good and bad, the yin and yang. However, the spectrum is leaning into darkness. In the absence of hope people do not care to do good, thus using their free will to do as they wish even evil deeds. Can't you see and feel it happening?" He looked into the blank stare on their faces, and although most of the gods were

200

The Great Gathering of Gods Soul

sympathetic to the human condition, they still had no answer as to what to do. The evil gods sat silently with smirks of joy for man's unrest. He slapped his hands face down on the podium.

Trying to get through them, he said, "Through understanding there is unification. It was only when I sought out the peaceful means in which others worship your name that I saw the truth of your being. After all, who are we to say, as individuals, that you appear to all nations as the same God? Perhaps you appear in a way that is acceptable to each nation and people, so that each people can accept you? Perhaps you adjust the same stories to fit the location and the people? But you are the same God! Are you not?" He stared into the crowd and there was quiet. They refused to answer. Not one of them said a word as if it were a sacred secret.

"ANSWER ME!" he said with harshness.

He waited a moment for a reply, but none came. Then, in a whisper, he was solemn and said to the gods, "Your silence is no longer good enough. We no longer need your books, churches and steeples. It is your help we need. It is the truth that only you can tell to set it straight. Please help us, God." His heart felt plea went out and some of the gods heard and seemed touched by his cry for mankind. Others noticeably did not care. Perhaps they felt they were too lofty to reason with a mortal man.

He stood at the podium staring out into the window view of darkness and destruction. There were no beautiful holographic images, like in the garden, to cover up the mess outside from the room of all truth, the Highest High. So, he said, "It is true, the way is always unfolding. The Qur'an says, 'We are all returning.' We are all stopping into this 'Tavern,' a kind of glorious hell in which mankind enjoys and suffers. Then we push away our stool from the bar at the 'Tavern,' in search of truth, as the human soul turns to find its way home. You must help me, also, because I, too, am a very old soul and I also want to go home."

As he said those words, he felt a pull in his heart that he had not allowed himself to feel before. For he had so much

The Great Gathering of Gods Soul

saving to do on earth that leaving man was not an option or even thought of until now. Still, he continued, "Rumi once said, 'If I could taste one sip of an answer, I could break out of this prison for drunks.'"

He pondered the quote and then asked, "Are you all One? One Godhead separated into so many pieces we cannot count in order to be with all of your people everywhere, for all time? If so, will you soon release us from the prison of our unknowingness? What will you do?"

There was no response, and he was not surprised. The council then took formation, surrounded him and escorted him out. As they walked down the corridor with burgundy red walls and rode down the elevator, he absorbed the day's questions, and then he noticed these strange men and how their formation seemed almost spiritual. It was strange but spiritual in the way they moved in such formation without missing a step. It was a dance that surrounded him, and while he was inside their dance, he was safe. Their diamond-shaped formation seemed to transmit information to him between the realms of intellectual and physical reality and of acceptance. Inside their shape he felt the strength again of his spiritual quest synthesizing his clarity of mind. He became forceful, unwavering, determined to manifest his goal to wake up the world from their sleep walk.

Other times when he saw them outside his door in the half hexagon, he felt as though they had created a window through which he could see beyond illusionary identities into the essence of the world he wanted to create. By watching their expressionless faces, he realized his own insecurities that made him divinely human and perfect as he was in his imperfection. He saw that the world was two direct opposites as he looked onto his council as the juxtaposition of himself. He learned through their non-expression that he would not hold back his expressions to the gods. He was willing to look honestly within himself to accept the truth. Whatever that may be, he knew that the gods had the power to create the truth they wanted to exist. The council had served as a mirror for him to reflect his inner thoughts through their physical reality and dance of silence.

The Great Gathering of Gods Soul

They, in fact, gave him support by confirming what he was capable of being and doing by their being and saying nothing. For in their silence, he had to look within himself for the answers and not listen to others.

He grew a profound affection for the men as they took those steps leading to his room for the night. For the first time, he felt honored to be in their presence instead of being annoyed. He understood why they were there with him and that he had been prepared for again in this way. To have the responsibility to speak to the gods, and while he was feeling alone, they were there all along. He learned to appreciate them and felt love for the strange men who had become his greatest allies. They were his stable point.

Chapter Eighteen

Day Six

Kingdom of Darkness

He stood in the morning glory from the window of his room, trying to forget that it was not real, and perceived the heat of the sun on his face, and it warmed his body while he thought of so many things. He felt such joy at being part of life and being aware of his appreciation of it. The sky was so blue as he watched the bird's work and play. He watched the plants and trees swaying with the ways of the wind. It was not only nature happening before his eyes, but it was a dance of the most elegant kind. It was life. To him they were like mankind, all different but all connected in the cycle of life. To him even dirt could rejoice in the morning glory without a doubt. He knew that minerals were full of atoms. Atoms in themselves were full of energy. Energy was intelligent, as he had learned in Asia while studying Reiki. He learned that energy seemed to move where it was needed and could heal when it was guided and directed to a specific place in the body. It gave life to nature through the sun, and it brought back life to those who were dying in their body or in their mind. He remembered that he had heard a scripture that said that God blew the breath of life into the nostrils of man. God called the breath of life, *life force*. Life force was no other than energy and when he learned that he could put intention into his life force for the sake of others, his energy became intelligent and so it was that everything to him was alive. Even though a rock was alive, the rock and plants did not have awareness of themselves so they could not appreciate their maker as he did. Satya knew that all mankind had the capability to be aware.

He understood that humankind were all at different levels of enlightenment, and it seemed that out of all the things they

The Great Gathering of Gods Soul

possessed, awareness was not one of them. Anyone could read a newspaper to see how man struggled with awareness and the knowledge that what he did affected others or caused a reaction in society. Where there was lack of awareness, there was lack of self-control. History had shown him that. Some were slow to learn, but it was there even if it lay dormant.

Perhaps, this is why some love whole-heartedly and some do not, he thought as he looked out the window, for he knew that love came with knowledge. He believed man experienced love fully when he understood the importance of diversity. He thought of Martin Luther King and thought of how love emanated from him because he had love for all people of every race and denomination. He only sought what was humane and fair as a human being. He did not hate those who persecuted him. He only loved himself and others and believed that all mankind were worthy of that same love of self.

Jesus, Buddha, so many others. They loved and did not exclude anyone from love. Those who didn't love seemed terribly miserable and filled with an inner hate mostly for themselves although they directed it at others. Hitler, who killed all those who were Jewish because they were of a different race, made sure to torture and starve them first. Pol Pot, was a man responsible for over one million deaths of Cambodians by executing them, starving them, by disease or hard labor. Sadam Huseein who was a vicious killer and dictator, who seemed like a scared and dirty puppy when found, and Osama Bin Laden, a mastermind killer of the masses. White supremacist groups hate anyone who is different but belong to something that feels like a family. There are homophobes who fear what they don't understand and racists of all kinds who are jealous or hateful toward any race of their preference, due to some personal affliction in their heart. How could anyone love fully when, in their own heart lies the leaven of insecurity and the fear that they themselves will never be loved by anyone? Their own fear of never achieving love makes them hate those who do.

He stood at the window and knew he was running out of time with the gods, and he wondered if he was making any

The Great Gathering of Gods Soul

progress at all. The gods had mostly kept their thoughts to themselves. He worried as he dressed and even when greeted by the divine council that escorted him to the Double Black Doors. For the first time he was anxious. His inner thought-world said, *They do not answer, and I do not know the great thoughts that enter their minds. Do they disregard the habitual utterances of an uneducated man with only clear sight? Disregard me they may, but they will hear me,* he thought to himself as he became more determined than ever.

He stepped into the Highest High with his beloved council behind him and approached the podium. To his surprise, he smelled the sweet smell of lavender and lilies and the tangy smell of the garden. It brought ease over him, and he remembered Jeziah's contentment and peace and Ke'ren's comforting words in the church when he was still a boy and smelled the same aroma of a garden. He knew that it was a sign of a blessing and so he began to share a story.

"Do you remember Icarus?" he said to the gods. "His father had such love for him that he made him wings of feathers held on by wax. His only warning to his son was not to fly too close to the sun. But Icarus was drawn to the light of the sun, so his wings melted, and he fell into the sea, the sea that is now called Icarian. So, it is Icarus who reminded me of mankind. Although we have divine instruction, we do not heed it and so meet our demise."

Many of the gods agreed with a nod.

"Is it kismet that we are drawn to that which ultimately hurts and destroys us? Is that part of this game of life?" Satya asked.

"There is so much that mankind has done to try to fix the damage they have done, only to have the goodness be perverted once more. There are hospitals to help those who are hurt, but only if they have money to pay for it or only if they carry the right insurance coverage. Insurance premiums are so high that the average man cannot afford them. Diseases are not cured for money's sake. For if there were no diseases, how would big business prevail? Pollution continues, although we have solar

The Great Gathering of Gods Soul

means. Parents are losing their natural affection for their children, abandoning them to grandparents or to no one at all. Governments no longer aid those who are trying to help themselves and still find themselves in need. The people try, they do. But in their efforts to achieve, they cause more corruption.

"There is nowhere for peace pilgrims to go. They are run out of society by big business and greediness. There are so many problems with this system of things that we would need a God of justice, a Forseti, on every corner to keep up. It is true enough that the Kingdom of Darkness opens its gates to everyone. But there is no darkness worse than the darkness that resides in the human mind!" he shouted, "the minds that create all this corruption."

"I am not an educated man. I am an autodidact who has learned everything he knows by the living of life, through pilgrimage, and the passion for goodness and peace. How can I seek teaching when I have always been the teacher? My methods are peaceful and direct. I am a transcendental soul whose foundation has always been truth. I have the gift of seeing things as they truly are and not as I would have them be. I would go to any length for mankind and look at their savior as my own duty. I will not tremble before it. There is nothing better for a warrior than a battle of sacred duty. A book called the *Philokalia,* of which I am fond, says, 'A master will often submit to disaster and humiliation for the sake of those who will benefit from him spiritually.' I have suffered at the hands of the ones I have saved through wisdom, for love's sake. You have bidden us to feel for our neighbor, have you not? But the people are desensitized and lack feelings of love and trust in this bitter world. There is little to afford in the way of softness, when surrounded by a world where people attack and kill one another through war, pollution, anger, disease and even extreme passion. Yet, there are those who still love others and are good. It is proof to them that you exist, although you have kept your silence.

"These questions of mine I drop squarely in the lap of God. That is who you are, is it not?" he questioned the gods.

The Great Gathering of Gods Soul

Some of the gods were insulted by his question and many shouted out, *"how dare you question us?"* The evil ones laughed while others, who felt they had done all they could, could care less.

"I have no more answers than the Great Sea of Man, yet I have one thing they do not posses" Satya said, "Unending love for them and faith in you that you will not falter. I believe that you can see the battlefield of our hearts and the torment of our conscience. Forgive us, Father, for we know not what we do."

The gods looked around to find *"he"* who uttered those similar words. The gods were touched by his plea and Jesus nodded in understanding with a tear in his eye. Nodding back, Satya posed a question.

"Isn't it true that those who have fallen in discipline live the reality of a world created by their own virtue? Even a sinner suffers his own fate and dwells in the ghetto of his broken-down heart until he believes in something worth living a noble life for. The Bhagavad-Gita says, 'The self is its own friend and its worst foe.' Is there a truer statement?

"I am not drunk with hypocrisy, pride or delusion. I have denounced desires and cravings for what seems to be centuries of fortnights ago. I wish now, and have always, sought enlightenment for the sake of others."

"If there is only one worth saving, will you not save the whole lot for that one? Would you not send out the Shepherd boy for the one lost sheep? I beg of you," he said. "I beg of you."

At that, the divine council began their formation around him and so he knew it was time to go. The room was quiet and the sky outside the windows was an eerie shade of gray. He turned from the gods with a slight, sad smile, and the council led him down the corridor and elevator to his abode where he did not eat but slept like the dead for the night.

The Great Gathering of Gods Soul

Chapter Nineteen

Day Seven

The Wheel of Suffering

Outside his window, it was pouring rain and the sky was black. The Hologram was gone. Without warning and quite startled, he was awoken by the sound of a presence entering his room. Although he looked, he saw no one in his half slumber. Still, he knew, like all the times before, that someone was there. Spirits had come to him in this way all his life. It was a gift he had been given. He sensed a presence of tremendous power and energy. What was before him was a powerful force and it came bearing symbols.

He did not know if he was a god or an angel. The spirit was frightening at first because he appeared like a wind of static blowing closer to him by the second. The spirit was powerful and intimidating as if he had thunder in each step that led him closer to Satya's bed. Satya gained his senses and asked him his name.

"I am Imlu," he said. In that same instant, he put in front of Satya's eyes hundreds of crystal symbols so beautiful and each one different from the others. Just like the ones that littered the ceiling of the Highest High. Then, Satya saw a golden wheel of some sort. It was so beautiful, but Satya did not understand. It was gold with engravings so masterfully done that it was clearly a work of art.

"I do not understand," Satya said.

"The truth is never obvious until it is known, Satya. But I will help you, my friend of greatness. The golden emblem that you have seen is 'The Wheel of Secrets and Suffering.' All men must look deep into the secrets of their heart to see what they hide. What hate do they hide that causes this great suffering on earth? Until they do this they will not know how to stop. There are beings that laugh at the suffering of man and no doubt you have sensed them in the meetings with you. It is they who implant endless amounts of data in these crystal images to trap and limit the spirit and body of mankind. Even in a body, man is as powerful as an angel. If only man knew that," Imlu stated. "There was a reason why you felt that eerie feeling the crystals gave you. Implanted data is everywhere feeding the self-conscious with negative thoughts and images," he said and then was gone.

With a bit more rest Satya woke to meet the day. He did not know what was to come that afternoon, but he did know that all he had said represented the people. All people everywhere. There was no doubt to him that man was imperfect. They suffer from things, big and small, mostly of their own doing. But the game had not been played fairly with them. That he must make clear.

As he looked at the Double Black Doors, he knew it would be for the last time he would address the gods. He entered and began his opening statement.

"Speaking to you has changed me somehow. It isn't as though my peace is gone, but I can't help but feel that you have been listening only partially as if with a deaf ear. You have said little to respond to my questions," he said as he looked around the room to address them all. "You are mysterious gods, so I wait patiently. I have thought about the things that we humans do to cause our own failures. It's true that we make excuses to justify our own crimes, behaviors, and our addictions. We blame others for our actions; create wagons to fall off of, and prisons to house the awful. All these things we can change or even redeem. Yet, it is so clear why we don't. Our failure resides in the blame itself. If we cannot first look inward, then how can we stop the cycle of that which we cause to occur?" he asked them rhetorically.

Then he explained, "In the effort to seek leadership, the people have relied on politics and religion for answers. Both make a mockery of your name. Politics rely on man to make the

The Great Gathering of Gods Soul

difference, but through his efforts, he has only made things worse. Religion has gone to such extremes that cults in your name live in confines, preach extremism, hurt children who are innocent to badness, stealing their childhood, stealing the means of living from its members, and still there is worse. In their effort to be holy and dominant, the religious go against their own doctrine of *Thou shall not judge* and judge their brothers. They condemn, even threaten their fearful followers for not agreeing or for having their own peaceful way. People are fleeing from these institutions and would rather be godless than take part in such groups.

Politics is an institution that never proclaimed you as their leader; religion, had you but lost you somewhere along the way when it became more about glory and wearing the name of God as if it were a badge of honor. Others use your name for themselves to lessen the value of others, as if your name gives them that right. So, on the journey alone to find you, many have become wise teachers, dai-ko-myos, senseis, buddhas, mahatmas, and healers. Their only goal was to show man that he, in the absence of love leadership, could become his own guide. Many have sought you earnestly and have become like dewdrops shining in the morning sun. In joy, they have taught acceptance, responsibility and to love thy neighbor. In the absence of scriptural text, they have put you, God or the idea of God, in their hearts and have taken it with them and passed it on through their teachings. There is still love in mankind," Satya pleaded. "We are all different but the same. We all suffer, and we all want love. It is love that gives mankind a reason to live. It is all our reasons," he said and then stopped. His tone then changed to one of a more solemn sound.

"In this game, there is so much suppression that people are losing their desire to live. Surely, this could not have been your intention?" he asked sincerely.

At last, the voice of a god named Mitra asked him, "What is it you want us to do, Satya?" Mitra was a Vedic god of light, who maintained universal order and justice and had the power to form friendships and contracts.

211

The Great Gathering of Gods Soul

Satya replied, "I want you to end this morbid game. I want you to listen to the cries of your people and know that it is your game that causes this. I want you to stop sitting idly watching them destroy themselves. Forgive me for saying, but I want you to show us the love that all your holy books say you have for mankind. Do you still have it despite the great badness on the earth because we have doubt?" he asked. "People are losing their hope in you and without hope, there is nothing. Without the people, there is no game for you to watch," he said.

"Then let us destroy this game with all its people," said Baal, Iblis and his cohorts of fear and destruction. Satya heard various shouts saying, "Let's cause their skin to peel from their bodies, to become sick and die from illness, or plague the earth with petulance and disease, far greater than what we have done thus far to cause them all to die." And they laughed. Another demon shouted out, "We have listened for days to you speaking with no resolution. You waste our time with your idle chatter."

"We have given you leadership and look what your people have done?" Another demon god named Hirayakashipu shouted. "They do not obey and so they destroy themselves. We are not to blame for your hell," he said with venom.

"True it is," Satya said. "Leadership has been given. But to give such young souls leadership who do not possess deep wisdom and expect them to rule a nation explains why their leadership has the earth constantly teetering on the brink of destruction. It was your plan all along, was it not, gods of evil? Only you could give us leadership that could not possibly lead when they themselves are blind! It is YOU who have implanted blasphemy into the minds of the people to stop their search for God. Their hearts wish to love God, but you have tried to instill a block to that love, love that is their birthright. How could it be blasphemy to seek out God's name in every place it might be found? Seeking only causes understanding of others and draws us to love one another more deeply. Understanding how others love God in their own way is good," he said.

"In my eyes, YOU are only here as a courtesy," he continued with disdain, "to ensure that there will never come a

The Great Gathering of Gods Soul

day that any one could ever say, 'that ALL the people of the world were not represented here today by their own gods.' YOU are not worthy of the hiss of a snake. As misguided as your evil and negative people are, the people who worship you and gather in your name only shows that such followers, even of evil, have an innate desire to connect with the virtue of family. They too want to be part of family, which was created by a loving God; that which you are not. You are just tokens of his kindness, allowed to still draw a breath and be, unconditionally. You are vile to me and the cause of all this pain and suffering," Satya exclaimed, looking at those whom he could see in the eyes. Anat and the others snickered at him while some seemed to come under his command. Iblis and Satan became quiet and watchful of Satya as if studying what he would say or do next.

Satya turned his attention to where there was love in the room. "Dear gods, I come to you with a question only you can answer. What will you do to solve these problems?" But as he looked into the eyes of so many gods, even those he had never heard of, he saw that many of them would not make eye contact with him, while others seemed to have pain in their eyes as though they had already reached their verdict.

There was no response or even a feeling he could grasp of some desire to change. For the first time in his life, he felt hopelessness. There was no response, just silence, just deafening silence. He had said every word he knew to express the condition of the world. He had been honest and up front with no fear of the consequences. It was he, a young man from nowhere who had stood up to scold God. Still, even in God's silence, he stood there loving and praising their names but for the first time he felt nothing in return. He felt blackness in his heart and the shocking feeling that death would be preferable than to go on living with the knowledge that God did not care. He wondered why he had spent all this time speaking before such greatness, only to hear silence in the end.

"If you do not care then, maybe ending this world is the only way. For I would rather die a tortuous death then to go

The Great Gathering of Gods Soul

back to the masses to preach that God does not care," he said fiercely.

"KILL ME NOW," he shouted at them, "As I wish not to be a part of a world without love and light. YOU have failed ME, a Nobody! It is you now who does not take your responsibility for your hand in our suffering."

At his disrespectful tone, the rumbling of voices began, and the words of the gods' backlashes filled the room to a fevered pitch. They all began yelling and cursing Satya's name for his reproach upon them, and they stood from their chairs pointing their fingers at him and some promised him torment. Some of the gods even threw their chairs across the room with violent anger hitting others gods and many fought back. The laughter of the evil gods mixed with the anger of the gods whom he had once revered and came to a roar so loud that it pained Satya's ears. He had never before felt such destruction of his entire spirit. If the gods themselves did not care, and those who did could not agree, then how could the gods ever expect the masses to follow them in peace? He wondered how he could not have seen their carelessness all his life. *Was everything I stood for a lie? Did I live all my life denying pleasures of the flesh and suffering for nothing at all?*

All this at once was enough to shake his sanity. Who was he and what did he stand for now? He had always known before. The noise of the gods was so loud that he could not hear anything but the screaming, so loud that he felt a painful sting from his ears. He touched the sides of his ears and there was blood dripping down his face. With a broken spirit and a sadness, he could never describe, a flood of tears came for his sorrow of these great leaders who were not great at all. He did not understand how it was that they could not see beyond themselves. The chaos in the Highest High was no different from that of the world.

He held his face in sorrow and the total despair that came with the loss of being unable to save his generation and the next. Then something miraculous happened. The gates of *Black Waters* opened up and flowed from his eyes. So much that the gods

The Great Gathering of Gods Soul

began to fall silent one by one as they felt the water touch their feet. The water of his tears was for the sadness, no longer for the people, but for them. So much *Black Waters* came from his eyes that it had touched the toes of all the gods. The room came to a hush as they—one by one—realized that what they were witnessing was a miracle. Just as Jesus fed the crowd on a single loaf of bread and turned a barrel of water into wine, love could make an empty person full of life once more. All that it required was someone who cared.

A dead silence occurred. The flow of water ceased from his eyes, but his heart still bled. It was time that he said what he had come there to say. The gods were now listening.

"There are still myriads of Noah's out in the earth," Satya cried. "We WILL NOT betray them. A promise was made, you gave a rainbow as your promise, and you WILL honor it!" he firmly. Again, the roaring of voices began with no union. He expected more from such great gods, together in one room. Still, he heard talk of destroying such kind people for the sake of some who were no good. Talk of flooding them again, burning them with fire, deceiving them and tricking them into gas chambers or giving them boils on their bodies and disease. All of these things that had been their ways in the past and his heart turned from sadness to rage.

Satya leaned his face toward the gods as if he could breathe fire on them like a dragon and there came a holy explosion from his mouth.

"I AM TIRED OF ALL THIS KILLING." But it was not just Satya's voice; it was the voice of all the people, male and female. All his glorious people and he felt Jeziah's face and spirit blend with his.

His firm statement was so fierce that the walls shook and released rubble. The gods began to ask each other who he thought he was to speak to them that way. Yelling and screaming commenced, and they hurled reproaches at one another. He heard various gods shout, "I am the ruler of the world. Not you." "I am the almighty King of Heaven." "I have more followers than you." He heard shouts of the devils saying

215

The Great Gathering of Gods Soul

in laughter, "I have won, I have won." Then, as it has always been for Satya, it happened once more. Complete peace came over him in chaos. He raised his voice above their screams.

"DO YOU KNOW WHO I AM?" he said as the glory of who he was came upon him and his total memory returned. In that moment, the gods looked confused and uncertain. Were they who they thought they were? Or were they?

Then, before his podium, there appeared the spirit creatures called Seraphim of times before the world's creation who were stationed before God's throne in the Heavens. They were the *Burning Ones,* on fire with Gods glory and protection. The gods eyes squinted at the sight of them, and they turned away from the Seraphim's shocking brilliance and glory.

"Go home, you gods. I am disgusted with you," he said. "Go home."

At that, the divine council bowed before Satya as he turned to face them to leave. He saw them prostrate before him and his throat tightened with love for these men who acknowledged his words and what he was trying so hard to do for mankind. One by one, the council rose to their feet and took their place in the diamond formation that Satya was waiting for, and then they led him out. The Seraphim stayed behind piercing the gods with their fiery eyes until Satya had completely exited the room of greatness. Then, as quickly as they had appeared, the Seraphim just simply ceased to exist.

The gods were witness to such honor bestowed upon him, and as he exited the Highest High for the last time, Satya felt their sudden twinge of fear. They did not know who they were.

The Great Gathering of Gods Soul

Chapter Twenty

Seventh Night

Awareness

Each god sat in his seat in confusion, some still struggling to maintain their power. But still, they could not help but wonder about what had just happened. Their thoughts were filled with confusion and chaos. The man spoke with such power. There were no words to describe him. Each god in his chair sat in silence going over the day's events and all the things that were said by this young man. Satya struck in them a fear they had not known in a long time because they had looked back at all their deeds and rulings to find that they had only made things worse in their attempt to fix the world. Their deeds had not been ruled by love or compassion for others but by the desire to rule supreme, by their desire to be glorified in vain.

They began to speak to one another. "Why did he ask, 'Do you know who I am?'" Benten, the deity of good fortune and happiness asked. Each god sat and thought about the question. The gods began to speak out loud to one another.

"Was that a question that we should ask ourselves?" Shiva, the god of creation asked.

With doubt and regret, the gods spoke randomly, "How can we be what we say we are when we do not help the people? When do we sit idly by while we hear the calls for help? We allow the attacks on their spirit and turn a deaf ear to the screams."

Another god added, "We judge and do not help them find us."

Still another god added, "They are not rats in a cage, but have we treated them as such. Have we been more consumed with the game we enjoy watching than with love and caring?"

Then questions began to come from every direction from all the gods.

"Have we sought after our own desires at the expense of others?"

"Were we cruel and unloving to the people that needed us the most?"

"Did we disappoint the people to whom we made promises too?"

"Did we abandon our children and mistreat them?"

"Did we lead them or were we too busy with our own sense of power that we forgot the little ones we were meant to care for?"

"Dear God," one shouted, "have we trampled on your children?"

The power of love, regret and tears of folly filled the room and the combined divine power of the gods silenced those who were wicked, and they ceased to speak and were tremulous. Then the last frenzied question went out before the crowd.

"What have we done and who are we if not the gods we thought we were?"

The cry went out from the gods, and it was heard.

Then suddenly, all the gods heard a voice from the heavens reply:

"Dear friends, I am not angry anymore for what transpired today. You were like the cats in the garden of the Vajra that believed they were wolves howling at the moon. You were given a gift to lead people but in your quest to lead them you lost your task and followed you own desire. You made your spirit larger than that of others. You betrayed your people who needed your loving support. They did not need you to be God as all beings are gods. They only needed you to listen to them and care. But through your selfish desires, you came to believe you were God Almighty. You believed that you were the one mover of the universe and thus began to fight for your dominance. You

ALL created wars and attached the words *Holy* or *Freedom* to justify your killing."

"You judged others and began to fight your neighbors. You forgot that all mankind was put on the earth, not one over the other! If you are all in existence, could you not see all were put there and given the breath of life? But you decided for yourselves what was right and oh, how wrong you were. For in your quest for dominance, you began to kill one another, destroy and pollute the earth in wars, cause illness for the sake of money and power. You lost your natural affection for your children and rejected any who had imperfections. You separated yourselves from each other and chose a different name for God if only for the reason of being unique and separate. Yet, God is not interested in vanity. It does not matter what his name is, or what he looks like. It is only mankind that is consumed with such things. Nothing has come into existence if it had not come through knowingness."

"There is no reason to hate, there is no reason to judge. There is nothing wrong with seeking God and leaving no rock unturned. He is not only in a church, a bible or in a cross. He is not anywhere, he is everywhere. He is not anybody, he is everybody. You my dear friends, you are not only a part of God, but you are also God. You are a drop of water that flows into a river. And in that river there is knowingness. Awareness of self beyond what you could imagine. But please try."

"There are only two truths in this universe. I am, and I create," he said. "Everything else is a lie." As they heard the gentle voice of Satya echo in the heavens, they spoke to each other of all the days they had given audience to God himself who came to save them and had not known. They were covered with the black veil of darkness and could not see what the truth was and finally began to realize it. They spoke of how they had seen themselves so far from one another and separate, but as they became present of mind they came to see the truth and realized that they lived on a pogost, a sanctuary of holy ground, where ministers of peace comfort the needy. There was not one pogost, church, or temple, but many, many pogosts, churches

The Great Gathering of Gods Soul

and temples. Each one, his neighbor, but they could not see beyond themselves to notice that they all shared a sacred task in ministering to the people. The black veil of their darkness shielded them from love, kindness, compassion and truth. All of which made life worth living. They realized that there was more than one way of looking at the world.

Looking out the window of the Highest High, the gods witnessed the black smoke of destruction disperse, seeing Satya's hands clear away from the world all that was destroyed so that they may begin anew. He forgave the world their harshness, as true love keeps no account of the injury, is long-suffering and kind. And what was left was the orange and yellow sky he had loved so much, showing the hope for mankind's future. They all agreed in conversation amongst themselves that a man could be blind even with his vision.

Are you?

"I have said, you are gods, and all of you are children of the Most High." — Psalms. 82:6

The Great Gathering of Gods Soul

"Careful how you treat one another. For, you may be entertaining God himself and not know." — Sufani

The Great Gathering of Gods Soul

The End

Sufani Weisman-Garza

The Great Gathering of Gods Soul

Symbolism Significance

Satya – Perfect knowledge and awareness of the actual condition of things, Truth

Crystal emblems – Implants put in the body to control and limit its force, to   make one believe they are body does not spirit and to trap a being in the body

Satya in the garden – Man in the Garden of Eden

Jeziah – God's feminine counterpart (Feminine of Jezreel, meaning "God Will Sow Seed")

Jeziah's garden – Garden of hope and selflessness

Garden Dome- Life is an illusion of what we choose to see

White cat in the garden of hope – Represents love and light always present. Female essence of God.

Black cat in the garden of hope – Represents the "Black Night of the Soul" that all human beings go through in their suffering. Male essence of God.

The Howling of the Cats – The spirits cries of suffering

The Cats exit of the garden – Life's pain is transitional

Seven days of meetings – Seven days of creation

2:00 A.M. – A mystical time of the body's energy rejuvenation process and factually, the hour most documented as the time of death.

Satya's age - Thirty-three years old – the age in which Jesus died, symbolizes what happens after his death. The conclusion. Thirty-three is the number of rest and calm

The man on the bench in Siena (sharing his marinated beef and peppers)-Good Samaritan

Siena mansion gates- false kingdom, unhappiness

The Tavern – Spoken of in the Qur'an as a place for souls to shelter before they move on to pursue truth

Highest High – Holy Ground

Double Black Doors – The Gates of Heaven, entrance to the spirit world

The Great Sea – Mankind

Forseti – God of Justice and Peace

Imlu– God of Humanity, Spirit Guide

Half Slumber – The mass sleepwalking of mankind through life

Dai-Ko-Myo – One who seeks enlightenment for the sake of others

Reiki- Ancient healing technique using touch to channel energy through the hands to heal others ailments, mental, physical or spiritual. Used even by Jesus

Golden Wheel of Suffering – The reflection of self, mans greatest or worst achievement

Black Waters- an eye condition of glaucoma used metaphorically as the blindness of the world, or *black tears* representing mankind's cry from darkness

Orange-and-Yellow Sky – Hope for the future of man

You Are Loved!

Place of Bliss Academy
www.PlaceofBlissAcademy.com

The Great Gathering of Gods Soul

Printed in Great Britain
by Amazon

26117078R00126